LIMITLESS SUPPLY

New Economy in the Digital Era

LIMITLESS SUPPLY

New Economy in the Digital Era

Chunsheng Zhou
Cheung Kong Graduate School of Business, China

Xiuhai Hu
Peking University, China

NEW JERSEY • LONDON • SINGAPORE • BEIJING • SHANGHAI • HONG KONG • TAIPEI • CHENNAI • TOKYO

Published by

World Scientific Publishing Co. Pte. Ltd.
5 Toh Tuck Link, Singapore 596224
USA office: 27 Warren Street, Suite 401-402, Hackensack, NJ 07601
UK office: 57 Shelton Street, Covent Garden, London WC2H 9HE

Library of Congress Cataloging-in-Publication Data
Names: Zhou, Chunsheng, 1966– author. | Hu, Xiuhai, author.
Title: Limitless Supply : New Economy in the Digital Era / Chunsheng Zhou, Cheung Kong Graduate School of Business, China, Xiuhai Hu, Peking University, China.
Other titles: Wu xian gong ji. English | New Economy in the Digital Era
Description: New Jersey : World Scientific, [2022] | "[Wu xian gong ji: shu zi shi dai de xin jing ji], originally published in Chinese by Citic Press Corporation, Copyright © Citic Press Corporation, 2020"--Title page verso. | Includes bibliographical references and index.
Identifiers: LCCN 2021047938 | ISBN 9789811247156 (hardcover) | ISBN 9789811247163 (ebook) | ISBN 9789811247170 (ebook other)
Subjects: LCSH: Technological innovations--Economic aspects. | Business enterprises--Computer networks | Electronic commerce. | Scarcity.
Classification: LCC HC79.T4 Z4813 2022 | DDC 338.064--dc23/eng/20211001
LC record available at https://lccn.loc.gov/2021047938

British Library Cataloguing-in-Publication Data
A catalogue record for this book is available from the British Library.

无限供给：数字时代的新经济
Originally published in Chinese by Citic Press Corporation

For any available supplementary material, please visit
https://www.worldscientific.com/worldscibooks/10.1142/12547#t=suppl

Desk Editors: Nimal Koliyat/Thaheera Althaf

Typeset by Stallion Press
Email: enquiries@stallionpress.com

Printed in Singapore

Foreword: New Economy Calls for New Theories

I am glad to write the preface for Professor Zhou's new book *Limitless Supply: New Economy in the Digital Era.*

The past few years have witnessed the booming of a new economy symbolized by smart and digital technologies in China and the world at large. New economic forms have changed how we live our daily life, how businesses are run, and how the macro economy is operated. Traditional economic theories can no longer illustrate the many new phenomena and problems emerging in the new economy. It is therefore inevitable that this new digital era is witnessing the emergence of innovative new theories.

Professor Zhou's new book is grounded in his theoretical exploration and innovation on the new economy. This book is a pioneer in illustrating the limitless supply in the digital economy — Microsoft's operating system, Tencent's WeChat, and Baidu's search engine (a Google-like search engine service) can be regarded as limitless supply products. When a product reaches the level of limitless supply, major changes are destined to occur in how its manufacturer prices, profits, and grows. Due to this limitless supply, new economy businesses can get rid of the capacity constraints of traditional companies and can achieve user-driven fission-type growth without heavy asset investment.

I strongly believe that readers would benefit a lot from this new book.

Liu Wei
President of Renmin University of China
July 10, 2020

Foreword: Limitless Supply: Theoretical Innovation in the Era of New Economy

First, I would like to congratulate Professor Chunsheng Zhou and Professor Xiuhai Hu for writing such an excellent and relevant book.

As I began to read *Limitless Supply: New Economy in the Digital Era*, I could not put the book down until I had read it through. The reason is simple — the topics in this book echo the ideas that I have and the concepts described answer many of the questions upon which I have pondered.

A good book seizes the opportunity and even foresees the future. The current era we live in features advanced technologies and innovations that have and will continue to change our lives and how the economy is developed and operated. Resource scarcity is the core assumption in traditional economics. Classic economics textbooks suggest that production is the transformation of resources into products, and the relationship between input and output is usually described by certain production functions: limited resource input results in limited output. More importantly, production by enterprises is characterized by increasing marginal cost and decreasing marginal output, which defines the shape of the supply curve. However, as we usher in the era of new economy, the resource scarcity hypothesis, along with all the theories on production as well as demand and supply derived from it, have been overturned.

New technologies and new economy have given birth to innumerable cases of zero marginal cost. For example, copying a program from one computer has a negligible cost; the investment Google and Baidu need to make to gain a new user for their search engine service is insignificant. At the same time, the new economy also contains several cases of increasing economies of scale — a social application becomes more valuable as the number of its users increases. Technologies such as these have gone beyond the limitation of increasing marginal cost and have ushered in a new era of limitless supply. *Limitless Supply: New Economy in the Digital Era* analyzes these new technologies and the new economy, and its timing is perfect.

Limitless supply is considered a symbol of an era; however, clarifying its significance as well as the new problems it brings to our social life, economic growth, and corporate management remains a challenge. Undoubtedly, limitless supply has led to many free products and services and made our lives much better and more convenient. From a macro perspective, limitless supply products in the field of new economy have made it difficult for economic growth theories based on production functions to reveal the inherent law of new economic growth. In addition, the current System of National Accounts (SNA) centered around gross domestic product (GDP) can no longer accurately summarize the contributions of digitalization and technological innovation to economic growth. On the other hand, from a micro perspective, enterprises offering limitless supply products with zero marginal cost drastically differ from equivalent traditional ones in terms of how they run their business, price products, and their profitability and development.

This book contains both theories and cases. The two authors have provided in-depth, systematic, comprehensive, and meticulous answers to many questions in a patient manner, which can help social managers, economic practitioners, and enterprises managers gain a deeper and clearer understanding of reality and the future potential. Several brand-new insights proposed in this book, such as asset intangibility, user capitalization, and digital monopoly, are worth paying attention to and pondering over.

Wang Yijiang
Professor of Economics, Associate Dean of
Cheung Kong Graduate School of Business
July 8, 2020

Preface

Amidst the inevitable upgrade of China's economic engines, the new economy continues to advance ceaselessly, along with the ever-emerging new technologies, products, and business models represented by smart and digital technologies. In this new era of economic revolution, the business community, financial world, and even the political circles are desperately seeking brand-new theories on economics in a bid to interpret the unexpected phenomena and problems occurring in economic activities, predict economic and business trends, as well as guide all walks of life to make more reasonable decisions on investment, R&D, production, and marketing.

Economics has been, for quite a long time, a subject that delves into economic patterns and resource allocation based on the scarcity hypothesis. According to traditional economics' scarcity hypothesis, production is a process that consumes limited resources, which leads to limited productivity and further scarcity of products. Nevertheless, the era of new economy has ushered in quiet yet rapid changes. While productivity and supply of some products remain limited, others have gone in the opposite direction — limitless productivity and supply — a trend that cannot be ignored. Microsoft's Windows operating system, Apple's iOS, Tencent's WeChat, Baidu's search engine, and many other products are typical examples of limitless supply.

Just as classic Newtonian mechanics cannot accurately explain particle movement, the theoretical framework of traditional economics centered around limited resources and supply can by no means precisely illustrate limitless supply in the era of new economy. Today, booming new business forms, such as smart economy and digital economy, are bringing about increasingly diverse limitless supply products. It is clear that it is time to think outside the box and establish a brand-new theoretical system.

However, there is no such thing as an easy job.

After years of pondering over and contemplation, we finally decided to compile this book to share our insights with the public.

The book analyzes and summarizes the basic features of limitless supply products and further compares the differences and similarities of how limited supply and limitless supply products are manufactured and marketed. In doing so, the book proposes the reasons why manufacturers of limitless supply products create intangible assets. The reason for this is that the scale of an enterprise producing limitless supply products depends on the user, whereas the scale of an enterprise producing limited supply products depends on the production capacity.

Combining the status quo of China's economic growth and features of the new economy era, this book explores how technological innovation, new economic patterns, and limitless supply influence a country's GDP. For example, the book clearly points out that the contributions of new economy and technological advancement to national economy are seriously underestimated.

This book is mainly written to construct a preliminary, simple, yet relatively comprehensive economic theory framework for limitless supply and to interpret the phenomena and corporate behavior in the new economy field.

Based on this, the book delves into how limitless supply products generate profit and gain derivative benefits by analyzing the demand and pricing of these products. As a result, readers can learn how limitless supply products, such as software, data, and online games, create balanced pricing, and why traditional products are rarely free and limitless supply products are mostly offered for free — zero prices or even negative prices.

Besides the insights mentioned above, this book explores how enterprises providing limitless supply products grow financially and further proposes the fundamental difference in growth models and rates between enterprises providing limitless supply products and those providing limited supply products, as well as the reasons why and how the former achieve fission growth.

This book also tries to answer other relevant questions, including competition strategies and user stickiness. Undoubtedly, the limitless supply sector enjoys distinctive features in these respects. Their unlimited supply breaks through the shackles of production capacity that confine traditional economic areas, thereby enabling enterprises to prioritize larger user scale to achieve industrial monopoly — a job made easier for them — and treat cross-over competition as a daily routine.

Instead of mere theories, this book employs a basic theoretical framework and all sorts of actual cases to help enterprises put into practice these concepts. Thus, many typical and critical cases and phenomena of new economy, such as zero return and negative return, "e-connoisseur," and ecological circle, are described in detail.

This book is simply a first attempt to explain the limitless supply economics, and many problems remain that need deeper exploration. If you, dear readers, find any mistakes or errors in the book, please feel free to contact us.

This book is written in a simple style, making it easy for anyone without a professional knowledge of economics to read and understand. The more complex concepts — theoretical analysis and economics models — are included in the appendix.

Finally, we hope this book can help business owners, enterprise managers, university graduates, and young entrepreneurs get better acquainted with the operation laws of new economy, enabling them to better navigate the smart and digital economy and other new economic fields. At the same time, we hope this book can catch the attention of the academic world as well as those interested in economics to further extend our studies and insights on limitless supply economics.

Chunsheng Zhou
May 4, 2020

About the Authors

Chunsheng ZHOU is a Finance Professor at Cheung Kong Graduate School of Business and a well-known economist in China. He received his Ph.D. in economics from Princeton University in 1995. Since then, he has held positions in various institutions, such as the Federal Reserve Board, University of California at Riverside, University of Hong Kong, China Securities Regulatory Committee, and Peking University. He has published numerous articles and books both in English and Chinese and has received several academic awards, including the prestigious China National Excellent Young Researcher Grant. He has made some original and fundamental contributions to the research on digitalized economy in recent years.

Xiuhai HU, a sociologist, is a distinguished researcher at the multicultural education research center of Peking University. His research interests include urban and rural development, culture and education, social issues, and economic reform in China. He has published several books on China's economic and social hot spots which help readers to better understand the current situation and development trend of Chinese society, and the system, mechanism, and function of the Chinese economy.

Acknowledgements

In early 2020, the COVID-19 pandemic, a major disaster swept across China and the rest of the world. People's work and life were disrupted and so were my work and teaching schedule. Fortunately, I had more time to sort out my thoughts and views on the economic issues that China is facing, especially the development of new economy, and I could finally sit down and write this book, which I hope is beneficial for all readers.

We are living in an age of innovations and great changes. Many economic questions remain unexplained and new fields remain unexplored, both from a micro and macro perspective. Existing traditional economics and management science theories are unable to illustrate the brand-new era of new economy that we are living in today. Hence, by focusing on the brand-new notion of limitless supply, this book is a preliminary attempt to interpret the many new macroeconomic phenomena and offer a preliminary theoretical framework and instructions for enterprise operation in the era of new economy. Many questions and concepts raised and proposed in this book need to be explored and discussed further by other scholars of economics. If you, dear readers, friends, professionals, and scholars find any mistakes or errors in this book, please feel free to share your valuable comments with me.

I have used some of the content in this book in lectures that I have conducted at Cheung Kong Graduate School of Business (CKGSB) for the Executive Master of Business Administration (EMBA) and Financial Master of Business Administration (FMBA) courses and shared the same with entrepreneur friends, students, and alumni of CKGSB. As I publish this book, I would like to sincerely thank CKGSB for supporting my studies and teaching work, my friends for their inspiration and assistance, and the people from CITIC Publishing House, especially Kou Yiming, for their valuable suggestions and corrections. I would also like to thank Mr. Li Lufei, the founder of "Zhen Zhi Zhuo Jian (Insight)" app (a learning platform focused on financial knowledge) and Ms. Wu Xiaoyu, Dean at Empowerment University, for their help and to my family for their loving care, while I was busy writing this book.

I would also like to thank some of my friends at Peking University and some of the students there (I do not know if they have graduated yet) who helped me with the book, including Dean Wu Zhonghai, Professor Feng Ke, Doctor He Li, Doctor Li Da, and students Guo Yucheng, Wang Zhiliang, Ding Bosen, Chen Yachen, Qiu Wenrui, Liu Wenhang, and many others. In the process of writing this book, a young yet talented student, Yu Zi'an, helped me collect and organize the materials. I wish to express my heartfelt gratitude to all of them.

I also referred to many publicly available materials that I found online and have cited research conducted by several scholars, especially for the cases that I have listed. I hereby extend my sincere thanks to all the authors and providers of all these valuable materials and data. I would also like to sincerely apologize for any mistakes or omissions in the citations.

Chunsheng Zhou
Beijing
May 3, 2020

Contents

Chapter 1

New Economy Driven by Innovation and Digitalization

Demand Creation and New Consumption in the Era of Smart and Digital Economy

Demand provides the original impetus for creation and economic growth. Material consumption now accounts for an increasingly smaller proportion in total social consumption, while "healthcare, education, and entertainment" consumption, propelled by the booming new technology and new economic models, has moved in the opposite direction.

Every economic activity is designed to serve the public by satisfying or creating consumer demand. If technology and innovation are the engines of modern economic growth, then our consumption demand and desire to improve life quality are the steering wheels. The former control the speed, while the latter point towards the direction.

In the huge yet intricate modern economic system, people usually categorize the business forms of enterprises based on who they serve. Producing and selling the means of production to business entities is called 2B (to Businesses); producing and selling consumer goods to people and families is called 2C (to Consumers). Both, in fact, are just a division of labor in the industrial chain. All enterprises, irrespective of what they produce — raw materials, intermediate goods, investment goods, or consumer goods — and irrespective of who they serve — other enterprises or consumers — fundamentally aim at satisfying consumers' demands. Consumers, therefore, hold the controlling baton of enterprise operation, as they are the fundamental determinants of the entire industry chain ecosystem.

Taobao, an eBay-like online shopping website, has brought about enormous convenience to production and life. But how did it overcome the barrier of online payment? As an e-commerce platform, Taobao created Alipay — its own third-party payment platform — to tackle the then incomplete e-commerce ecosystem where there was a lack of trust in payment providers, and there were limited options available. Hence, this shows that social demand is the largest driving force of innovation and corporate growth.

There are many levels of human needs. Abraham Harold Maslow, an American psychologist, organized human needs into a hierarchy of needs — a pyramid with five levels (from the lowest level to highest) — physiological, safety, love and belonging, esteem, and self-actualization. Each need, though profuse at each level, differs greatly. For example, in "physiological" need, food is the basic need for survival. Poor people may just want to fill their stomachs, but the rich seek delectable tastes and healthy meals. A single meal, going by this idea of hierarchical needs, may then cost you anywhere from RMB 10 to even RMB 10,000.

With economic development and technological innovation, people's needs continue to evolve and sometimes become new demands that were earlier either unimaginable or considered impossible. That is the reason why people today care a lot about demand creation. Demand creation means that market entities stimulate our potential demands and satisfy them through various means of production and operation with the help of new technologies, products, services, and business philosophies. For example, the creation of airplanes stimulated the need to travel on long journeys by air to destinations they may not have thought of previously. As most people in the world have access to digital technologies and mobile internet, and emerging social applications like WeChat, Facebook, Tik Tok, and Weibo (a Twitter-like microblogging website), we have started to telecommute, and the rise of online education has inspired people to pursue education on the internet.

In an era when technological level and economic development lagged, people only had low-level needs of food, clothing, shelter, and transportation. Building on this, even now, when we talk about consumption, our first thought is towards life necessities.

The rapid rise of Artificial Intelligence (AI), big data, and mobile internet has not only brought us several brand-new industries, products, services, and business models but also stimulated unprecedented consumer demands, and disrupted our traditional consumption concepts. At present, there have been radical changes in how we spend money and what we spend money on. Now, more people prefer to spend more on entertainment, leisure, healthcare, tourism, education, culture, sport, social service, and information service. To summarize, modern people need "clothes, food, shelter, travel, healthcare, education, and entertainment." To be more specific, "healthcare" refers to health and wellness, "education" refers to learning and culture, "entertainment" refers to recreational activities, leisure, and travel in general. These three aspects are the future engine for consumption upgrade and growth.

In brief, "clothes, food, shelter, and travel" are subsistence- or material-driven consumption, or rigid demand; while "healthcare, education, and entertainment" are development- or enjoyment-oriented consumption, or non-rigid demand.

Ernst Engel, a German statistician and economist born in the 19th century, proposed an economic law based on his studies on consumption structure: The poorer a family, the greater the proportion of its income (or total expenditure) that must be devoted to the provision of food. As a household's income increases, the percentage of income (or total expenditure) spent on food decreases. This can be extended to whole countries, and thus, the poorer a country, the greater the proportion of per capita income (or average expenditure) that must be devoted to the provision of food. As a country gets richer, the percentage declines. In professional terms, the income elasticity of food consumption is between 0 and 1. It is called Engel's law.

As a society advances, material consumption takes up an increasingly smaller proportion in total social consumption, making room for the rapidly growing consumption of "healthcare, education, and entertainment" propelled by the booming new technology and economic models — a practice of Engel's law in consumption structure. As shown in Fig. 1, from 2012 to 2017, China's consumption structure experienced drastic changes — the proportion of food, clothing, and daily supplies in total consumer spending plummeted, while transportation and communication, education, culture, entertainment, and medical care, excluding the huge number of free services (e.g., free voice chat, video call, and WeChat social entertainment), brought about by the digital economy and technological innovation, soared.

After China proposed the great historical mission of building a moderately prosperous society in all respects, new technologies, including AI and robots, have been extensively applied in production and our daily life,

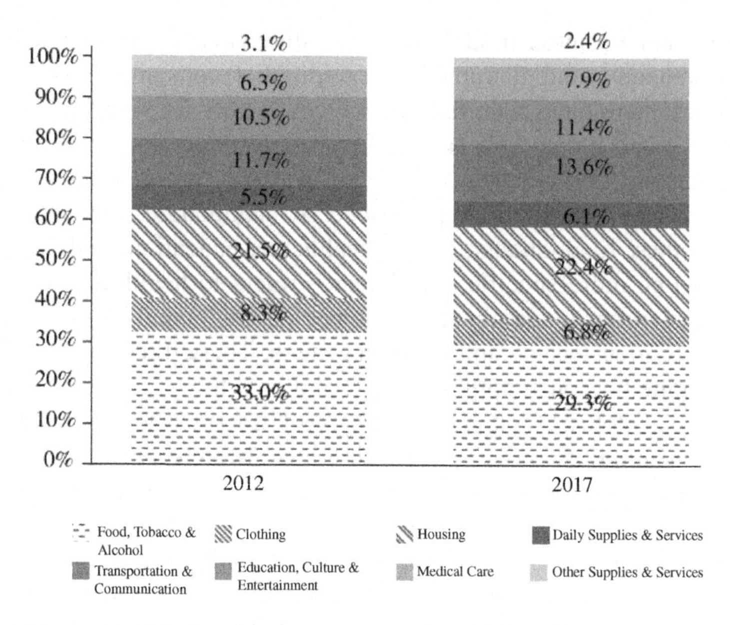

Fig. 1 Changes in China's consumption patterns from 2012 to 2017.

Source: Youth.cn, March 16, 2018.

and the average life expectancy has steadily increased thanks to improved medical services and healthcare. It is predicted that people will have more time and energy to pursue higher life quality — traditional consumption fields, including "clothing, food, shelter, and travel," are further refined, while "healthcare, education, and culture, as well as leisure and entertainment" have become increasingly popular daily routines of the public. From the demand side, traditional consumption fields are being combined with smart applications, and new ones rapidly rising from "healthcare, education, and entertainment" are and will continue to be key growth points of China's economy. We call these new demand-side economic increments.

New Economic Increments Driven by Digitalization and Innovation

The robust development of China's new economic formats represented by the rising digital economy is attributable to the driving force of technological progress and innovative models, as well as to the upgraded economic engine and structure.

On February 14, 1946, the world's first general-purpose computer (GPC) "Electronic Numerical Integrator and Computer (ENIAC)" developed by the United States Army was announced to the world at the University of Pennsylvania. This marked humanity's and the world economy's entry into the information age. Since the 1990s, especially since we stepped into the 21st century, digital technology has been developing rapidly. Digital and smart technologies, represented by e-commerce, mobile payment, new media, big data, AI, Internet of Things (IoT), and industrial internet, have extensively penetrated all aspects of life, including commercial trade, industrial production, business management, public administration, national security and defense, financial transactions, people's livelihood, cultural education, journalism, and communication. In other words, the entire world, especially major economies like China and the United States, has entered a new age of smart and digital technology.

At present, the Chinese economy is known as the new economy. Generally, the term "new economy" refers to an economic model driven by an information technology revolution, against the backdrop of economic globalization, and features high-tech digitalization and smart technologies. The rapidly progressing and widely adopted smart and digital technologies, in turn, not only facilitate production, trade, and information exchange but also greatly reduce transaction costs and information asymmetry. What is more, they have even triggered numerous new products, business models, and economic formats, such as drones, self-driving cars, robots, shared mobility, big data marketing, intelligent information service, online group buying, online education, and social networking service.

As shown in Fig. 2, in 2000, among the world's top 10 most valuable companies, Microsoft was the only one specializing in internet software. In 2010, Apple, another digital economy company from the United States, joined the list. In 2019, a total of 7 digital economy companies — 5 based in the United States (Microsoft, Apple, Amazon, Google, and Facebook), and 2 in China (Alibaba and Tencent) — now filled up the list.

Although China is still a developing country, it has reaped the fruits of a digital and smart economy, and is a large global player in the digital economy, second only to the United States. China's AI has also taken the lead in global R&D.

1990		2000		2010		2019	
Japan	Nippon Telegraph and Telephone Corporation	USA	Microsoft	China	CNPC	USA	Microsoft
Japan	Bank of Tokyo-Mitsubishi UFJ	USA	General Electric	USA	Exxon Mobil	USA	Apple
Japan	Industrial Bank of Japan	Japan	NTT Domoco	USA	Microsoft	USA	Amazon
Japan	Sumitomo Mitsui Banking Corporation	USA	Cisco	China	ICBC	USA	Google
Japan	Toyota Motor Corporation	USA	Walmart	USA	Walmart	USA	Facebook
Japan	Fuji Bank	USA	Intel	China	CCB	USA	Berkshire Hathaway
Japan	Dai-Ichi Kangyo Bank	Japan	Nippon Telegraph and Telephone Corporation	Australia	BHP	China	Alibaba
USA	IBM	USA	Exxon Mobil	UK	HSBC	China	Tencent
Japan	UFJ Bank	USA	Lucent	Brazil	Petrobras	USA	Johnson & Johnson
USA	Exxon Mobil	Germany	Deutsche Telekom AG	USA	Apple	USA	JP Morgan

Financial investment | Communication & hardware | Internet software | Petroleum | Mass consumption

Fig. 2 Top 10 world's most valuable companies in the past 30 years.

Source: www.zhihu.com.

From 2010 to 2019, China's R&D expenditure kept increasing at a compound annual growth rate (CAGR) of around 18%. In 2018, China spent a whopping RMB 1.97 trillion on R&D, 2.18% of its GDP, and the number of R&D personnel and patents both ranked the first in the world.

In 2019, the strategic emerging industry, science and technology service industry, and high-tech service industry all achieved double-digit growth — around 12%, in terms of operating revenue. The added value of the strategic emerging industry, to be specific, captured a larger part of China's GDP each year, approaching the target set under the national plan for development during the "13th five-year" period. By 2020, it was expected to reach 15%, thereby elevating the emerging industries into economic pillars worth "RMB 10 trillion."

A study published by the Shanghai Academy of Social Sciences in 2019 suggested that in 2016, 2017, and 2018, China's digital economy grew by 21.51%, 20.35%, and 17.65% year-over-year (YoY), respectively, ranking first in the world for three years in a row, higher than any other country, including the United States. As per the *Digital China Establishment and Development Report* (2018), in 2018, China's digital economy reached RMB 31.3 trillion — a YoY nominal growth of 20.9% on a comparable basis, accounting for 34.8% of GDP, which included RMB 6.4 trillion of digital industrialization — 7.1% of GDP. In addition, the software and information technology service sector, and the internet industry saw YoY revenue growth of 14.2% and 20.3%, respectively. At the same time, industrial digitalization surpassed RMB 24.9 trillion — a nominal YoY growth of 23.1%, accounting for 27.6% of GDP. The added value of industry, service sector, and the agricultural digital economy took up 18.3%, 35.9%, and 7.3%, respectively.

Figure 3 depicts the dynamics of China's digital economy since the 21st century, highlighting the role of digitalization in China's economic growth. At the beginning of the 21st century, the digital economy was just in its infancy; since 2010, it has moved on to the fast track. So, by any measure, the digital economy is playing a critical part in China's economy.

Broadly speaking, in 2019, the digital economy sector in China employed around 190 million people — 24.6% of total employed population. A year before, in 2018, the digital economy had already contributed 67.98% to China's economic growth. Now, the digital economy has become a strong pillar of economic growth, as well as a beacon lighting up the future.

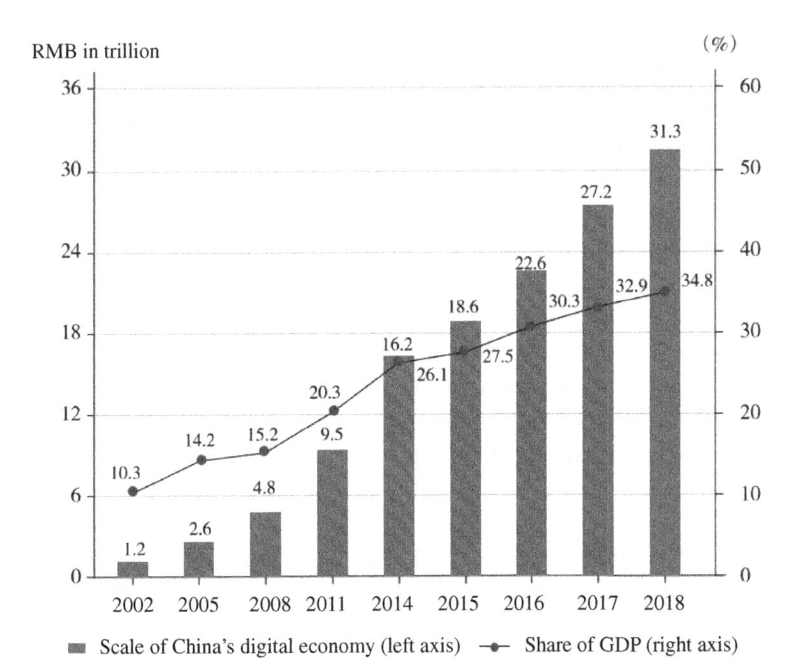

Fig. 3 Growth of China's digital economy.

Source: https://www.sohu.com/a/312895996_473133 Qianzhan Industry Research Institute: Analysis on China's digital economy market in 2019: Promoting the transformation and upgrade of relevant sectors in response to global digitalization transformation, May 9, 2019.

The booming new economic formats represented by the digital economy can be attributable to the driving force of technological advancement and innovative models, as well as to the upgraded economic engine and structure in China.

The first three decades of high-speed economic growth after China initiated the reform and opening-up policy were mostly brought about by rapid industrialization propelled by a large labor force, low costs, and relatively limited material products. After years of rapid economic development, the process of industrialization and related capital accumulation has pretty much reached the zenith. Traditional markets, including real estate, basic manufacturing, low- and middle-end product export, and basic public consumption, have gradually saturated, leaving little or no room for growth. As a result, the economy, companies, and consumption all need to make brand-new breakthroughs and seek incremental space for growth. But where can we find this space for growth? The answer lies in innovation, in ground-breaking technologies and products, and in creating new demand.

In the past decade, China has achieved exceptional results in the digital economy, AI, robots, drones, biotechnology, and quantum technology, laying a solid foundation for the transformation and upgrade of the national economy, and pointing the way forward for enterprises to seek new growth opportunities. China will not stop here; it will continue marching ahead with innovations and further development.

Digital and smart economy has not developed through a marginal improvement of technology or superficial economic restructuring but through a great revolution in production, distribution, and lifestyle. Compared with the first industrial revolution triggered by "steam power" and the second one powered by "electricity," the current technological revolution, represented by digital and smart technologies, has had a profound influence on all aspects of life.

Why is the Acceleration in Technological Innovation Leading to a Deceleration in Economic Growth?

Potential opportunities for economic growth, what we call new increments, will continue to pop up in emerging industries like the internet, data technology, AI, and new energy. A growing new economy can undoubtedly improve our production model and lifestyle. However, many new economic formats have not contributed, as well as traditional industry and manufacturing, to quantitative indexes like fixed assets investment and GDP.

As we mentioned previously, China witnessed obvious progress in technological innovation and new economic formats in the past few years. China is catching up with the United States and other superpowers in science and technology, especially in the digital technology, AI, and communication. Another critical fact worth pondering over, however, is that while China keeps striding forward in terms of technology, its economy is clearly slowing down. So, why is this happening, and what to make of this relationship between the two? In order to answer this question, let's first look at how China's economy has progressed since the reform and opening-up.

At the 3rd Plenary Session of the 11th Central Committee of the Communist Party of China (CPC) in December of 1978, the policy of "internal reform and opening to the outside world" was initiated. Since then, China's economy has taken off. The internal reform started in rural villages. In November of 1978, Xiaogang Village, Fengyang County in Anhui Province, initiated the household contract responsibility system (commonly known as "an all-round contract") by dividing farmland into households and having them assume full responsibility for their profits and losses. In urban areas, state-owned enterprises (SOEs) gained a lot of managerial decision-making autonomy. In July of 1979, the CPC Central Committee officially authorized Guangdong Province and Fujian Province to implement special policies and flexible measures for foreign economic activities, making headway in reform and opening-up. Thus, "opening to the outside world" became a basic national policy, paving "the path to a stronger China," and working as a strong engine for advancing the socialist cause. What's more, reform and opening-up helped establish the socialist market economy. In 1992, Deng Xiaoping, the chief architect of reform and opening-up, gave the important "south tour talks." He illustrated the basic principles of a socialist market economy and started a brand-new chapter for China's reform and opening-up as well as modernization. In 1978, China's GDP was RMB 367.87 billion, and GDP per capita was RMB 385, ranking 134th in the world, almost at the bottom of the whole list, behind less-developed countries like Zimbabwe, Rwanda, and Haiti. In terms of GDP per capita, China was then only 0.4% of Monaco, 1.47% of the United States, and 1.77% of Japan. Although China ranked first in population, its GDP was only 6.3% of the United States, 14.7% of Japan, and 20% of Germany.

After the reform and opening-up in 1978, China's economy grew at a breakneck speed. The possible reasons for that are as follows:

First, a large working population escaped the shackles of limited rural land and swarmed into cities, providing abundant and relatively cheap labor for the rapid industrialization of cities. They gave strong support to the early manufacturing industry — low-end manufacturing, in particular, provided a significant cost advantage for Chinese products, which debilitated international competition, and further facilitated foreign trade, especially export trade of industrial products.

China's high-speed economic growth was also driven by "high investment." Generally, a higher rate of gross fixed capital formation (GFCF) — the share of GFCF in GDP — is a feature shared by the miraculous economic growth of many Asian countries and regions. Take Japan for instance. Japan's economy boomed from 1953 to the 1970s thanks to its nearly 35% GFCF. Singapore, during its economic boom period from 1971 to 1985, had a GFCF exceeding 40%. Malaysia, too, experienced a few years of the economic boom in the mid-1990s, due to its over 40% GFCF at the time.

Many western economists think that a relatively high GFCF and large-scale investment were the two major engines for China's high-speed economic growth. They think that investment, one of the engines, was not only from domestic deposits but from many direct foreign investors as well. The reason is that several foreign companies rapidly entered and invested in China to capture the vast domestic market and the cheap and abundant labor force. According to the World Bank, China's actual utilization of foreign direct investment increased from USD 630 million in 1983 to USD 60.3 billion in 2005 — a 15% growth each year on average. As of the end of 2005, China had used USD 618 billion. The big rush of foreign capital not only propelled economic growth but also made great contributions to enhancing China's technological advancement and export competence.

Second, the cheap and abundant labor force guaranteed China's rapid economic growth. According to a report released by the Organization for Economic Co-operation and Development (OECD), China enjoys comparative advantages that no country or region in the world can match.[1] The first one is the abundant labor force. China provides nearly 10 million

[1] Quoted from China enjoys comparative advantages that no country or region in the world can match, wenku.baidu.com, December 15, 2011, author: weishu520.

more jobs every year, and over 150 million surplus workers in rural areas are waiting for employment in cities. The other one is that such a high-quality labor force comes at affordable prices.

Third, higher efficiency accelerates economic growth. The improved technologies and labor skills, in turn, enhanced efficiency and total factor productivity (TFP). On the one hand, as China transformed from the once rigid planned economy to a flexible market economy, production factors were reassigned and applied in departments or areas of higher efficiency. On the other hand, direct foreign investment brought sufficient capital as well as technologies and management experience, all of which are critical factors in improving TFP. In addition, as China advanced in education, the quality of the working population rose tremendously — another obvious reason for higher TFP.

Fourth, the rapid increase in international trade pushed China's economy forward at a high speed. Since 1980, China has always treated foreign trade as a key factor that drives and aids economic growth. In doing so, the Chinese government gave up some administrative rights on international trade, lowered trade barriers, and sought to join the World Trade Organization (WTO). Thus, China's international trade took up a greater proportion of the world's total volume of trade year by year.

Last, structural reform laid a solid foundation for high-speed economic growth. A key to rapid economic growth is an efficient structure whose efficiency derives from a property system that stimulates economic entities. Undoubtedly, reform of the economic structure offered a strong impetus for China's growth in economy and productivity.

At the First Plenary Session of the 18th CPC Central Committee in November of 2012, Xi Jinping was elected General Secretary of the CPC Central Committee. Also, that year, China experienced major Changes in its economic development mode and economic growth speed. The quantity-oriented GDP turned to middle- or high-speed growth centered on high-quality and sustainable growth.

"China's development is still in a significant period of strategic opportunity. We must boost our confidence, adapt to the new normal based on the characteristics of China's economic growth in the current phase and stay cool-minded,"[2] said President Xi during his visit to Henan Province in May of 2014. It was the first time a CPC central leader used

[2]*President Xi illustrates "new normal" for the first time*, xinhuanet.com, November 9, 2014.

the term "new normal" to describe China's next period of economic growth. Under the new normal, China's economy has slowed down significantly in accordance with the current GDP indexes, but it is on a path of higher quality.

China's GDP has slowed down under the new normal. In short, after years of high-speed development, traditional industries (we call them stock industries) have accumulated a large capital scale and productivity. As Engel's law suggests, the large product demand of traditional industries cannot keep growing rapidly and steadily, thus an imbalance has emerged between supply and demand, and some industries have even experienced excess capacity. Opportunities for further growth are quite limited for such stock industries.

In the future, chances of rapid economic growth will appear mostly in emerging sectors like the internet, data technology, AI, and new energy. A better new economy can significantly improve production methods and lifestyle, but comparatively speaking, many new economic formats do not contribute as well as traditional industry and manufacturing to quantitative indexes like fixed assets investment and GDP. The details are as follows:

(1) Stock industries like industrial manufacturing mainly grow due to equipment investment and capacity expansion. The new economy relies more on innovation and R&D on technology and models, and less on fixed asset investment like plants or heavy equipment. For manufacturers of limitless supply products, a larger scale is not due to expanded capacity backed by equipment and facilities. In the age of the new economy, a topic frequently mentioned by everyone is "asset-light model," meaning creating intangible assets. Intangible assets overtaking tangible assets are a key feature and trend of the new economy age, which has made the national economy less dependent on fixed asset investment.

    As shown in Table 1, in the past few years, fixed asset investment, especially private investment, has slowed down drastically. Before 2010, fixed asset investment in China maintained a growth rate of 25%. But ever since 2018, its growth has slowed to less than 6%.

(2) A robust economy has also expanded China's foreign trade. However, as China's comparative advantages in global industrial division shift, along with changes in global political and economic landscape, China cannot maintain a sustainable super high-growth rate for its foreign trade. In certain sense, a slowdown in its foreign trade is inevitable.

Table 1 Changes in the growth rate of fixed asset investment in China from 2005–2019.

Year	Growth over the last year (%)
2005	26.0
2008	25.9
2009	30.0
2012	20.3
2015	9.8
2017	7.2
2018	5.9
2019	5.4

Source: National Bureau of Statistics.

(3) The field of the new economy — in particular, the digital economy — has witnessed the appearance of multiple limitless supply products and services with zero marginal cost (the concept of limitless supply is elaborated in Chapter 2). They have ushered in a new era of free services, where consumers are no longer directly charged. Instead, they profit via other channels or methods from suppliers of products and services. However, the value provided for customers is yet to be fully included in the current GDP statistics; hence, the contributions from new economic formats to economic growth are underestimated by the current GDP indexes.

(4) Technological innovation, a key player in the new economy, is more clearly reflected in the improvement of the quality of economic growth. For instance, our computers and mobile phones have become faster, and cars and air conditioning have become more energy efficient. At the same time, the current GDP indexes are clearly more focused on quantity and not quality.

(5) According to the current GDP statistical caliber and method, as the new economy advances, especially as new products replace traditional products, the scale and level of economic growth will be seriously underestimated (refer to Chapter 3 for more details). The most obvious example is how GDP indexes fail to evaluate the impact of free limitless supply services that replace traditional paid services.

As a result, we think China's economic slowdown, or GDP slowdown more specifically, can be attributable to three reasons: First, the capacity of traditional industries (stock industries) is somewhat saturated compared to the demand (including foreign trade demand), and lacks sufficient momentum to keep advancing at a high speed. Second, new economic growth (new increments) sees a strong trend of intangible assets, thus relying less on fixed asset investment. Demand for investment, however, is a key part of GDP. Third, the current GDP statistical caliber and method underestimate the contributions of technological innovation and new economic formats to economic growth.

Trend of Future Economic Growth

Smart and digital technologies will continue to restructure China's economy, leading China and even the whole world to experience several major new trends.

New increments, smart, digital, and information technologies — as well as scientific development and model innovation symbolized by technological breakthroughs — are remolding the enterprise structure, production methodology, and operation philosophy, and reshaping work approaches, lifestyle, behavior, and habits. Therefore, we hereby make some preliminary predictions on the future economic growth based on smart and digital applications:

(1) The gap between simple labor and complex labor (intelligent labor) will continue to widen. AI and robotic technologies will take over most simple labor as well as some mental labor in the global market, forcing people to turn to more intelligent and creative jobs. This tendency will lead to reduced demand for simple labor, and a widening gap between simple and complex labor.
(2) For the same reason as previously mentioned, for outstanding enterprises, the quality of the labor force will easily prevail over quantity. All enterprises will compete fiercely with each other for high-end creative talents, leaving fewer job vacancies for simple labor.
(3) Smart and digital assets will become a production tool (factor) that is more critical than machinery and equipment. In the economic era dominated by manufacturing or agriculture, the most important production factors, as well as the key components of corporate assets, were land, factory, and equipment. In the era of a new economy led by creativity and smart and digital technologies however, R&D

achievements and digital assets will become the essential components of an enterprise's productivity, thus an "asset-light" structure of corporate assets. Specifically, a company's R&D achievements, technological level, and digital assets are its intangible assets. Therefore, the "asset-light model" is about creating "intangible" assets. Further details are discussed in the following chapter.

(4) With weakening information asymmetry and increasing transparency, consumers will be more demanding with respect to product quality, and users will have greater bargaining power against business entities. As a result, competition among enterprises will become fiercer, accelerating the survival of the fittest model. At the same time, higher transparency will reduce enterprise profits and further squeeze the profit margins of competitive products.

(5) Industries will be more concentrated, and many of them may be dominated by a few excellent companies. If there is no outside intervention (e.g., government), we will witness ever-increasing cases of oligopolies and monopolies. Monopolistic enterprises have superior client resources and crossover operation capabilities, and will hence find it easier to find the high ground in multiple related sectors.

(6) With the further development of the digital economy, the network will become ubiquitous and the IoT will also develop rapidly (Fig. 4). Everything will be interconnected (e.g., smart home, smart office, and smart building), and separated only by a closed intranet.

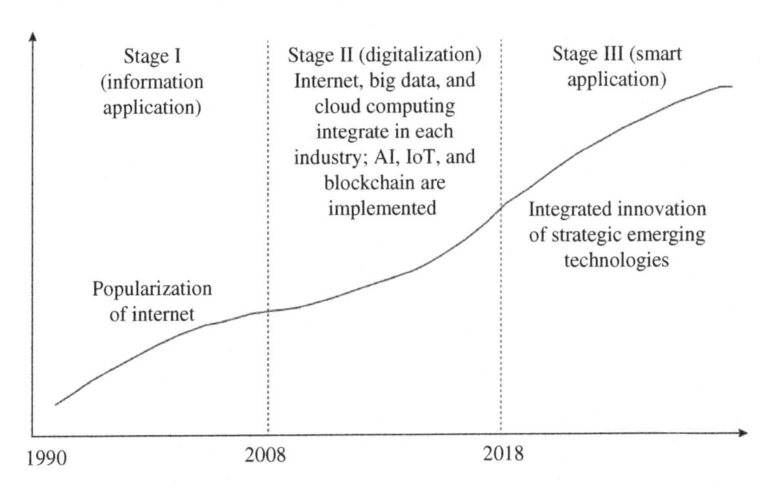

Fig. 4 Development history of the internet and digital economy.

Source: Public documents from sage ledger (www.hatdot.com).

(7) There may be limitless digital products, but the time available with people and their attention span are limited and fixed. Hence, enterprises will shift their focus of competition from production factors and market to users (traffic) and user attention — a valuable and limited resource.
(8) Restructuring of the industry chain will occur through technological innovation and increase consumer demand. In the past, the entire industry chain was composed of many stages, from production to consumption, and from producers to traditional dealers and then to the consumers. But in the future, consumer demand will come before production and supply; products will be designed first according to consumer demand and then manufactured. Traditional dealers will gradually fade away from the market.
(9) Rapid technological advancements will lower both the cost and price of technological products while boosting performance. Consumers, in turn, can spend much less for something faster and of higher quality. The big rush of limitless supply products will provide consumers with even more free services. What's more, lower cost boosted by advanced technology will also ease the pressure from inflation.
(10) The acceleration of information exchange and the rise of remote or distance education will narrow the knowledge and information gap among people. The widespread use of intelligent robots and AI technology will liberate people from heavy, simple, and non-creative labor, and the consumption of "healthcare, education, and entertainment" will continue to rise rapidly.
(11) Users of a new economy and digital products are not mere consumers anymore. They have become the assets or "part-time workers" of companies. As the new economy marches ahead, with a higher degree of product and service digitalization, users will play a more critical role as assets or workforce.
(12) Traditional consumption for subsistence will shift from being quantity-oriented to quality-oriented. Basic life necessities, such as food, clothing, furniture, general household appliances, and medicine, will see a slowdown in their growth rate, while products with higher quality brought by technological innovation and advancement will receive increasing importance. Besides, new consumption models created by new economic formats and technologies will overwhelm the market and serve as a key component of consumption upgrade.

Chapter 2

Limitless Supply Triggered by Innovation, Digitalization, and Technology

Traditional Economy — Scarcity of Resources and Limited Supply

The basic tenet of traditional economics is the scarcity of resources and limited supply. To grow and branch out, an enterprise must first figure out how to expand its capacity.

This book focuses on the large number of limitless supply products in the new economy as well as consequent market features and enterprise behavior. To make it easier for readers to understand the characteristics of limitless supply, which are later explained in detail, let's first take a look at an essential topic of traditional economics — the basic concepts and theories of limited supply.

As we all know, resource scarcity is a basic tenet and core assumption of traditional economics. The scarcity hypothesis means that resources, including land, labor force, raw material, and capital, can never produce sufficient products to satisfy humankind's unlimited desire (demand). For example, land is a limited resource, so we can never build enough garden villas for everyone to enjoy, nor grow enough high-quality grapes to create countless top-ranking and high-end wines such as the "Château Lafite Rothschild." Mines and forests are limited too, so we can never exploit sufficient gold or other resources to make countless amounts of steel or Chinese rosewood furniture. Human resources are limited, so we can never hire nannies for each family, to ensure every family enjoys greater comfort in taking care of their children.

Of course, the scarcity hypothesis mostly refers to relative scarcity, wherein a resource or resource type is scarce compared to people's present or potential demand. Consequently, it requires all social and economic activities to be carried out for the purpose of gaining maximum results at the cost of minimum resource consumption. Therefore, resource scarcity and the consequent human desire to maximize economic effects at minimum cost are why economics is an independent subject that is still being researched and studied today.

The scarcity hypothesis contains two hidden concepts. First, in a market economy, resource utilization is exclusive and competitive. In other words, enterprises need to pay for the resources they need and would seldom share these resources with others. Second, production consumes resources, hence limited resources can only result in limited products.

In a market economy, scarce resources are by no means free. The scarcer the resource, the higher the price. The total price of the resources consumed or utilized by enterprises for production constitutes the total production cost. Economists widely believe that, with a reasonable technological level, productivity can be determined by how many resources are being invested in. Economists usually use certain production functions, such as the Cobb–Douglas production function,[1] to describe the quantitative relationship between resource (or factor) input and the amount of output.

According to the general product function, to boost yield, the manufacturer must first increase factor input and cost. The added cost for each new output is called marginal cost of the corresponding product. The relationship between input and output is determined by resource scarcity and production functions, which means:

(1) Marginal cost must be a positive value and cannot be zero or negative. The reason is that higher productivity requires more factor input, thus more cost.
(2) An enterprise cannot add factor input without limitation. Thus, production volume must be limited, leading to limited supply.

[1]The most famous and widely used production function, proposed by two economists, Cobb and Douglas, in the 1930s.

(3) In the short term, some factors, such as factory and machinery, are fixed and cannot be adjusted. At the same time, to drastically increase productivity, the manufacturer can only add more variable factors, such as labor force and raw material, leading to an imbalance between fixed and variable factors, and thus cost increases faster than production volume. Economists call it increasing marginal costs, which in turn affects enterprises' enthusiasm to increase production volume.

If we call the optimal number of products that an enterprise can produce under the existing capital investment as production capacity,[2] then to increase capacity, the enterprise must add further inputs. So, in the limited supply economy, to grow and branch out, an enterprise must first tackle capacity expansion — to increase capacity by adding factor inputs.

What Exactly are Limitless Supply Products and Limitless Supply Economy?

Limitless supply products can be supplied simultaneously or in a short time, without any limit, at zero marginal cost to the manufacturer, to satisfy any market demand. In short, so long as there is demand, enterprises can provide as many products as they please.

In the age of traditional economy, most products, including food, clothing, cars, and machine tools, require huge human and material resources as inputs during production, only to generate limited production volume, which is in turn, decided by how much is invested.

Nonetheless, in the era of new economy, the production process and capacity of smart and digital products are fundamentally different. For example, Microsoft's Windows operating system and Office software, Apple's iOS, Google's Android, Tencent's WeChat, Alibaba's Alipay, Baidu's search engine, iFLYTEK's AI-powered voice recognition system, ByteDance's personalized information push service (Toutiao and Douyin), and AutoNavi's Amap (map service) are all fruits of labor, intelligence, and creativity of innumerable technical talents. These are the fruits of complex labor, according to Marxism, and are fundamentally different

---

[2]Capacity is normally interpreted as the maximum output level based on an enterprise operating its current production factors at full load.

from food, clothing, and cars. Smart and digital products can be replicated unlimitedly at nearly zero cost but cars and clothing cannot. For example, to produce one more car, the manufacturer must invest more human and material resources and equipment to run the production process again. However, systems and software, such as Baidu's search service and Toutiao's information push service, are not shackled by production volume. That's why we call them limitless supply products.

With the advancement of digital technology and the vigorous development of communication media, services that could only be provided to a few people in the traditional economy can be multiplied limitlessly without any added cost. Such services are also limitless supply products. For instance, a lesson taught in a classroom is only for dozens of people at most, but a lesson live streamed is for countless viewers. The same goes with concerts in a music hall or live streamed on a video website. Moreover, a live streamed video can be stored online and replayed countless times.

In terms of a relatively authoritative definition, we define limitless supply products as products that can be supplied simultaneously or in a short time without any limit, at zero marginal cost to the manufacturer, to satisfy any market demand. In short, so long as there is demand, enterprises can provide as many products as they please.

What needs to be pointed out is that limitless supply means a single product can be supplied limitlessly and not that an enterprise can supply countless different products. For example, a program, once developed, can be supplied without limit, but it doesn't mean the developer has countless software to offer. A song (digital music), once written, can be supplied without limit, but it doesn't mean a singer has to sing different songs countless times.

Obviously, limitless supply products are by no means scarce or competitive. Whether there should be any restrictions on the usage of such products is mostly up to the policies and attitudes of the suppliers.

Limitless supply products can be consumer goods, such as online games, digital music works, and mobile applications, or production tools and materials, such as computer numerical control (CNC) software for machine tools and enterprise or individual credit data for banks.

If the major products or factors of an economic system, once produced, can be supplied without limit according to demand, eliminating the traditional competitiveness, then such an economic system is called a limitless supply economy. In short, limitless supply economy is a system composed of limitless supply products, including copyrights, scientific and technological achievements, computer software, and digital products.

Sir Arthur Lewis, winner of Nobel Memorial Prize in Economic Sciences and Professor of Political Economy at Princeton University, proposed the concept of "unlimited supply of labor" in a famous paper published in 1954. A relatively backward developing country has extremely abundant labor force in rural areas; hence, modern industrial enterprises can access seemingly unlimited labor force based on how much these rural workers are paid (usually only sufficient to meet the minimum living standard). However, the unlimited supply of labor proposed by Sir Lewis is fundamentally different from the limitless supply concept in this book (we title this book *Limitless Supply: New Economy in the Digital Era* to differentiate from Lewis's book and to highlight that limitless supply products truly reach the stage of infinite supply).

First, unlimited supply of labor refers to the relatively excess labor resources, which, as industrialization marches ahead, also become scarce. However, limitless supply products or factors proposed in this book can be literally supplied without boundaries.

Second, from the supply-side angle, unlimited supply of labor is a macro concept. However, in the micro sense, each supplier or worker to be more specific, can provide limited labor power. But from the micro perspective, the suppliers of the limitless supply products can achieve limitless supply.

Finally, as Lewis suggested, unlimited supply of labor is priced exogenously — usually the minimum amount to barely make a living and the suppliers constitute a fully competitive market where no one has the pricing power. Meanwhile, limitless supply products are priced by suppliers based on the principle of maximum profit — an endogenous driving force; however, the suppliers usually have to deal with a market prone to monopolistic tendencies.

Science and technology is a productivity force. So long as we treat technologies (inventions and innovations) as a production factor, just like labor force, land, and capital, any achievement resulting from technological advancement can be supplied without limit, used repeatedly for countless times, and even provided for all target enterprises and individuals concurrently. Michael Faraday discovered the law of induction, which, no matter how people put it into practice, always remains unchanged. The Wright brothers invented the first airplane, and the design and manufacturing techniques, no matter how many planes we make in the future, are additional improvements based on the original design. Yuan Longping, a Chinese agronomist, created hybrid rice, and his findings, no matter how widely used, will always be objective scientific achievements. It is noticeable that technologies can be supplied without limit, but normally, a single technology cannot give birth to ready-made products for enterprises or consumers, as the raw materials and human resources are limited. Take Apple for instance. Its iOS operating system is supplied limitlessly, but the display screens, chips, batteries, and other components that constitute an iPhone are limited.

It's important to know that in the current era of digital economy, data can not only be directly provided to users as consumer goods but also applied in manufacturing and business as key production factors. Data, once generated, can be repeatedly used countless times by innumerable users — there is no competitiveness, hence supplied unlimitedly. In April of 2020, the CPC Central Committee and the State Council of China jointly published the *Opinions of the CPC Central Committee and the State Council on Improving the Systems and Mechanisms for Market-based Allocation of Factors of Production* (hereinafter referred to as Opinions) — an essential document of landmark significance — which included technology, data, land, labor force, and capital as key types of production factors in the new era. Interestingly, land, labor force, capital, and other traditional factors are supplied with limit, while technology, data, and other core factors of new economy are without limit. The difference is also demonstrated in their allocation mechanism. For instance, the ownership of land and capital remains effective over the long term whereas that of data and technologies requires a reasonable protection duration stipulated by relevant laws.

Fundamental Difference between Limitless and Limited Supply Products

For limited supply products, the scale effect is reflected on the supply side, and the expansion of the enterprise depends on its capacity expansion; whereas, for limitless supply products, the scale effect is reflected on the demand side, and the expansion of the enterprise depends on user growth. Limited supply products are competitive and suffer from damage and depreciation, whereas the limitless supply products can be used for multiple purposes at the same time and there is no depreciation.

Limitless supply products in the era of new economy usually require highly innovative R&D, for which enterprises need the appropriate R&D expertise and creativity and a superior talent pool. They also involve relatively high R&D cost in the initial stage. Thus, although enterprises providing limitless supply products don't need to invest much in fixed assets, such as machinery and equipment, or incur any follow-up marginal costs, they must still bear a large initial investment cost as well as relatively high risk due to market uncertainty.

Generally speaking, limited supply products consume limited resources that are available during production, involve marginal costs, and experience damage and depreciation. For example, bread, once eaten, can never reappear on the table; steel, once utilized, can't be reforged; and cars, once driven, require maintenance and repair every couple of years. But this isn't the case for limitless supply products. When limitless supply products are used, they are seldom damaged or depreciated; even in case of rare instances where such an event occurs, it doesn't matter much, as customers can replace these abundant products at any time as they please. Tencent's WeChat and Google's search engine, for instance, are supplied without limit and encounter no damage or depreciation.

Limitless supply products don't have marginal costs and no other cost is incurred by the producer in their usage. Hence, compared with vendors of traditional products, vendors of limitless supply products have greater flexibility in how they market their products, their profitability, as well as the pricing of their products. Traditional products, if sold at a price lower than the production cost, would result in a vicious circle of higher sales leading to a bigger loss. On the other hand, no matter how low priced a limitless supply product is, it will still generate some gross profit.

All enterprises create products to sell, or to be more specific, to make profits. However, before generating profits you need users for the products — key resources for every enterprise. However, limited and limitless supply products don't have the same dependency on user base due to the following two reasons.

First, for limited supply products, the user base determines the quantity demand, but the maximum sales cannot surpass the enterprise's maximum output, i.e., the capacity. If an enterprise can produce 1 million products per year, the maximum it can sell is 1 million products in a year. Even if it were to have 100 million potential users, it can only supply the product to 1 million of them. When the enterprise increases its product price, it ends up losing or wasting large amount of user resources.

Hence, the scale of limited supply product vendors depends on capacity or the supply side, at least in the short term. For instance, Maotai, the most popular liquor brand in China, enjoys a large customer base, but the product has had limited supply for many years. Maotai's production has never increased sufficiently to cater to the demand; it has remained around 40,000 to 50,000 tons per year, mainly due to insufficient production capacity.

For a limitless supply product, it is the supply side that decides how fast the enterprise can introduce products that perform well and have high quality. Theoretically, after the R&D stage, a limitless supply product can be sufficiently provided for each consumer without capacity constraints. At this stage, the number of users, or the demand side, is essential to determine the enterprise's scale.

Second, limited supply products have a relatively high and even increasing marginal cost. Sales must grow faster than the cost — the prerequisite for enterprises to make pricing and production decisions. Thus, limited supply product vendors cannot ignore costs while trying to acquire users. For limitless supply product vendors however, marginal cost is not an issue — even if they sell their products at an extremely low price, they can still generate profits as they have a large user base.

In conclusion, market share is of immense significance for limitless supply products. How much the enterprises can grow and expand is not dependent on the production capacity but rather on the potential user base. Thus, users become the fundamental factor to determine enterprise scale.

Comparatively speaking, the scale effect for limited supply products is reflected on the supply side and the expansion of the enterprise depends on its capacity expansion, whereas, for limitless supply products, the scale effect is reflected on the demand side and the expansion of the enterprise depends on user growth.

As mentioned previously, limited supply products, once used, can experience damage or depreciation, hence the usage itself is a process of consumption, a process that generates cost, and a process that is mostly competitive and directional. If a steel beam is used to build a railway track, then it can't be used to build a car; if a house is built as a residence, then it can't be changed into a factory.

But this doesn't apply to limitless supply products with digital technology. During usage, there is no need to worry about damage, and the products can be used for multiple purposes. Specifically, one product or platform enjoys multiple functions that can be used all at once without any conflict. For instance, WeChat serves as a social communication tool, a marketing tool, a payment and transfer platform, a game portal, an e-commerce promotion channel, as well as an e-media. On downloading and installing WeChat, end users become both the consumers and contributors who generate revenue, through advertising, financial services, and online shopping commissions, for Tencent. Therefore, WeChat is a product that satisfies end-users' social demands as well as a means of "production" that helps Tencent diversify revenue sources. On the other hand, the end users are consumers as well as the agents of Tencent's "2B" business. Based on this, Tencent allows users to download and use WeChat for free but still generates huge profits from it.

This proves that limitless supply products, including digital products, can have multiple functions that can be used concurrently, so that suppliers don't need to count on direct sales for revenue. If necessary, the enterprise can diversify profits via royalty on digital and smart products, licensing fee, advertising, and product promotion — so called derivatives. Intriguingly, revenues from derivatives may be much higher than direct sales revenue.

Traditional manufacturers of limited supply products, irrespective of how popular their products are in the market, can never get rid of capacity constraints. To grow and expand, a company must tap the market to attract more consumer demand and invest more human and material resources (equipment and means of production) on the supply side to expand capacity. But even if the entire process is done perfectly, it is still slow and requires both time and money. So, it is extremely difficult for traditional companies to grow exponentially, to achieve what we call fission growth today.

In the era of new economy, vendors of smart or digital products may need to invest a lot of money and time in early R&D to develop limitless supply products, but once they succeed in launching an outstanding product in the market, they no longer need to worry about capacity constraints. With the aid of the internet and new media, so long as enterprises are willing to invest in marketing and promotion, they can start from scratch and become a giant in a pretty short time.

Take Douyin (international version is called "Tik Tok") as an example. Douyin is a social application that was launched in 2016 but has experienced exponential growth over the past couple of years. Its parent company, ByteDance, branched out and became a nationally and internationally influential enterprise that specializes in social networks, entertainment, and media within three years. Pinduoduo, a third-party social commerce platform founded in 2015 and which focused on consumer to business (C2B), officially expanded into the US market in July of 2018 with a market capitalization of USD 24 billion. In August of 2018, Pinduoduo released its first financial report after listing — it had 2,489% YoY growth in Q2 that year. According to Pinduoduo's 2019 annual report and market value as of the end of April 2020, Pinduoduo is now one of the largest e-commerce platforms in China, bigger than JD.com (a massively large B2C online retailer in China) and Vipshop (a Chinese company that operates the e-commerce website VIP.com) and is second only to Taobao.

Details on fission growth model of manufacturers of limitless supply products in the era of new economy are delved into further in Chapter 6.

Overturning Traditional Economic Concepts

The production function used to describe the input–output relationship in traditional economic theories is of zero significance or reference to the supply of limitless supply products, as such products, once produced don't have their supply falling short of the demand and don't need to worry about market clearing.

Carl Shapiro and Hal Varian highlighted in their book *Information Rules: A Strategic Guidance to the Network Economy*: "Technology changes, economic laws do not." But we, the authors of this book, do not agree; we think the changes in technology also bring possible changes to economic laws or at least to some of them. Now, let's talk about the exact changes in economic laws during the shift from traditional to new economy.

According to resource scarcity hypothesis, production, a process that consumes limited resources, leads to limited production volume and limitedly available products. How scarce a certain resource is determines its price and the price of relevant derivatives. From a macro perspective, resource scarcity hasn't totally disappeared in the new economy, but in micro terms, it is no longer a tough challenge for limitless supply.

The output of traditional products depends on resource input, as one more product produced consumes one more resource. Producing smart, digital, and other limitless supply products (such as software) also consumes resources, such as labor force and energy. But such products, once produced, can be supplied unlimitedly as required without additional capital or labor force (except for sales force, bandwidth, and marketing expense). Supply falling short of demand is never a problem. The production function derived from traditional economics that describes the input–output relationship is valid for anticipating the production volume of cars, food, and clothing but not suitable or meaningful at all in describing the number of copies of software, data, audio, and video products.

In terms of scarcity and competition, brand-new production factors such as technology and data differ fundamentally with traditional ones such as land, capital, and labor force. The former are knowledge-based human creation that are always in short supply because from a macro perspective, as society continues to advance, it keeps creating more innovative technologies and data, which in turn require better technologies and data. However, from the micro perspective, any technology or data, once generated, will never be in short supply. Existing technology or data can be used constantly without depreciation or used concurrently by multiple companies and individuals. The current technology or data will not run out, irrespective of how many products you produce using them.

In brief, traditional factors such as land, capital, and labor force are in limited supply, whereas technology and data either don't exist as yet or are never in short supply.

The production cost is derived from the resources consumed during production. Traditionally, the more industrial or agricultural products we produce, the more resources we consume. Therefore, the total production cost increases along with the production volume. In limitless supply products of the new economy, although production requires a lot of human and material resources, once a product is produced, it can be multiplied without extra cost (Fig. 1).

Market clearing is of great significance to traditional industrial and agricultural products, as the total cost increases with the production volume — in other words, marginal cost is positive. When supply exceeds demand, the unsold products pile up, leading to wastage. Consequently, most enterprises choose to reduce output and/or price to relieve the inventory pressure. On the contrary, when demand exceeds supply, enterprises increase their mark up and increase profits by increasing production volume. In such a scenario, they further adjust their plans, ramp up investment, expand capacity, and eventually strike a balance between supply and demand — a strategy called market clearing.

Limitless supply products don't face this issue of supply not meeting demand as the vendors of limitless supply products can provide as many

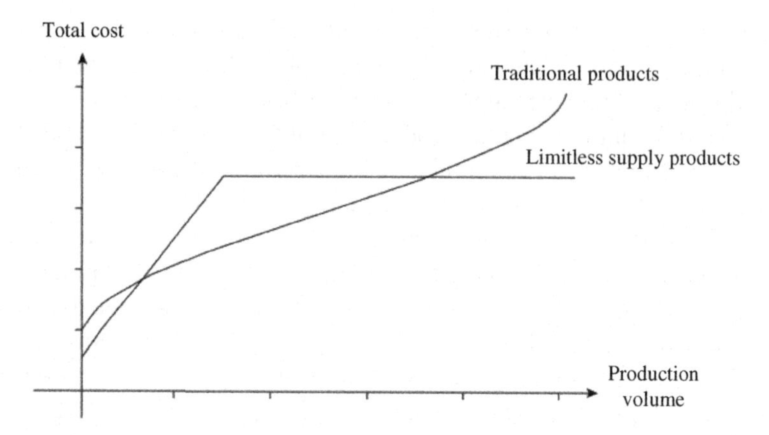

Fig. 1 Relationship between total cost and production volume of traditional/limitless supply products.

products as the market requires at zero marginal cost. Such vendors also don't face the issue of excessive inventory as there is only one product — unless they can't sell that one product. In addition, all the initial investment is the sunk cost. So, market clearing is unnecessary in the era of new economy.

Supply and demand never exceed or lag each other. The mechanism of striking a supply–demand balance via price regulation in traditional economics is no longer applicable in the market of limitless supply products. Microsoft, for example, doesn't feel the pressure of "surplus inventory" even if it doubles the price of its Windows operating system and its sales volume is halved; it also won't run into a supply shortfall with increasing demand even if it halves the price. In a different market environment, Microsoft can adjust the pricing of its products to maximize the profit, but such an adjustment does never arise from a supply–demand imbalance nor does for clearing out inventory.

Intangible Assets and User Capitalization

The term light assets can be interpreted as light fixed assets or light intangible assets. Successful new-economy companies, especially those focused on digital economy, usually posses many intangible assets, or we could say they are intangible-asset companies. For them, users (traffic) are the critical resources and are prioritized as their core assets.

Assets are resources that a company owns or possesses and that are expected to generate economic value. In the age of traditional industrial economy, enterprises mostly grew and developed based on their production capacity. This production capacity depends on how many fixed assets, including factories, machinery, and equipment that the enterprise owns. Therefore, such enterprises own so-called heavy assets relative to their sales volume. That is, in a traditional economy, in assembly manufacturing and heavy chemical industry in particular, most enterprises own "heavy fixed assets."

In the era of new economy, in the fields of AI and digital economy in particular, technical and innovation capability as well as business model determine the enterprise's market prospects. Such enterprises invest less in fixed assets, such as heavy equipment, machinery, and factories, as production capacity is no longer a factor now, especially for vendors of limitless supply products. The assets of such enterprises are mostly "light" — what we call "light assets" nowadays.

The concept of "light asset" has been widely accepted by the broader society, but logically speaking, it is not fully adopted. If an enterprise could easily grow into a large-scale enterprise, such as Toutiao and Pinduoduo or even behemoths like Baidu, Alibaba, and Tencent, it must have some unique core resources or core competitive advantages that can generate huge benefits. These resources are still companies' assets — in intangible form. Some intangible assets may be disclosed in the financial statements (balance sheet), whereas some others may be difficult to evaluate, thus not disclosed at all. But importantly, those not included in the financial statements, or undervalued, are still assets. So, "light assets" are actually light fixed assets or light tangible assets. Successful enterprises in the new economy usually possess many intangible assets, thus they deserve a more appropriate name — "heavy-intangible-asset" company or "intangible-asset" company.

According to Tencent's 2019 annual report, as of the end of 2019, Tencent owned USD 18.499 billion intangible assets, USD 8.844 billion real estate and equipment, and only USD 100 million inventory assets. The combined book value of its tangible assets was far below that of its intangible assets and accounted for only a small portion of Tencent's whopping USD 136.955 billion total assets. Given that most of Tencent's intangible assets are difficult to count or confirm, or nearly impossible to disclose in its financial statements, we can assume that the total value of its actual intangible assets is even higher than the number mentioned in the report.

The most typical intangible assets, in this age of new economy, are technology and data. Many modern companies, though being relatively weak in terms of total assets, rank high in market value and price-to-book (P/B) ratio.[3] The major reason behind this is the fact that intangible assets, a major part of their total assets, are not reflected in their financial statements.

For vendors of limitless supply products, as we mentioned earlier, users are the key resources, as their growth depends on a larger user base and not expanded production capacity. In the new economy, and the internet industry in particular, enterprises and users usually establish a long-term interdependency and don't just have "one-time-only" transactions. Once a person becomes an enterprise's user, he/she can then continuously provide revenue and profit for the enterprise. So, most enterprises spare no expense in attracting more users — a behavior called "cash burn." Companies spend lavishly to attract new users as, basically, users are the most critical resources for economic benefits in the era of new economy, especially the digital economy. Based on the definition of assets, users (traffic) are now regarded as corporate assets and are in fact the core assets (Fig. 2).

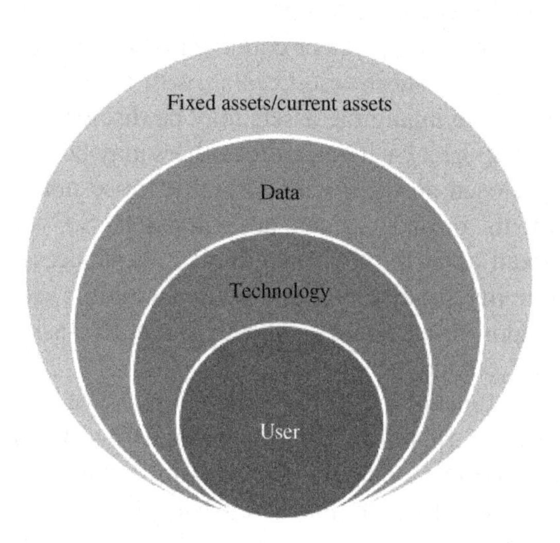

Fig. 2 Composition of assets of limitless supply product vendors.

[3]Financial ratio that refers to the ratio of a company's market value against its net assets; P/B in short.

Another reason to justify why users are the core assets is that the market value (estimated value) of vendors of limitless supply products is highly related to the user base.

China's internet-celebrity economy, which rose during 2014–2015 and experienced leapfrog development in 2019, is expected to surpass RMB 700 billion of total value in 2020. Profitability and social status of internet celebrities, especially the top-ranking ones, further illustrate how important users (traffic) are as core assets in the era of new economy. On the evening of January 5, 2020, Li Jiaqi, the Chinese live streaming celebrity, promoted a product "spicy sausage" on his live streaming channel. He sold more than 100,000 packets of the spicy sausage within five minutes, with the total number of viewers reaching 16.77 million, and generated huge live streaming revenues. A top internet celebrity earns more than an A-share listed company does in a year. How do they make so much money? Not through real estate, equipment, or investment but through influence, fans (users), and traffic. An internet celebrity, if treated as a company, only possesses one important asset — users (fans).

When a product or factor can be supplied without limit, then the capacity constraints are no longer a concern, and there is no risk of supply not being able to meet the demand, which is common in traditional economics. Limitless supply involves zero marginal cost of products due to which cost is no longer an additional factor to consider in pricing. Roughly speaking, digital and smart products are priced according to both their own value and the business models of the suppliers.

Chapter 3

Influence of Limitless Supply and Technological Development on GDP

Categories for Innovation in Economics

Innovation doesn't mean Pareto improvement. Innovation, while strengthening the competitive advantages of certain enterprises, weakens the competitiveness of their opponents, thereby reshaping the industrial and market structure. There are many types of innovation according to different criteria.

Innovation is the primary driving force of corporate development. In a market economy, besides educational and research institutions that are constantly driving technological research, market entities or enterprises are gradually taking an active part in technological development. Comparatively speaking, companies make practical and targeted innovations, as they naturally aim to capture the high ground in market competition to reap higher profits. However, innovation is a positive externality. Even innovations that are meant for internal benefit probably end up being altruistic and contributing to the broader society and economy.

It's worth pointing out that just because innovation is related to an enterprise's competitiveness, it doesn't mean it is about Pareto improvement. While strengthening an enterprise's competitive advantages, innovation weakens the opponents' competitiveness and reshapes the industrial and market structure. When an innovation becomes revolutionary and can generate a brand-new product or service or provide products or services at a much cheaper cost or in a more convenient manner to replace existing suppliers, it can somewhat overturn the current market structure. For example, cellphones replaced pagers and digital cameras replaced film cameras. History proves that enterprises, including large enterprises, who are unwilling to revolutionize and oblivious to ground-breaking technologies will decline or even go bankrupt due to the loss of market and users.

There are many types of innovation according to different criteria. In this book, we put innovation into the following categories based on how innovation influences production, transactions, and other processes:

1. *Innovation that improves means of labor*: Such innovation involves new machinery, new production tools, and equipment that have higher performance and efficiency.
2. *Innovation that enriches objects of labor*: Objects of labor refer to all the materials to which human labor is applied. Innovation and technological development enable us to choose richer, better, and cheaper objects of labor.
3. *Innovation that multiplies product features*: It's the most common innovation, seen in terms of improved clothes, cellphones, computers, TVs, air-conditioning, cars, and home furnishing materials.
4. *Innovation of new products and services*: Technological innovation keeps enriching material and cultural products, such as drones, intelligent robots, facial and voice recognition, automatic translator, mobile payment, and stem cell therapy.
5. *Innovation in transactions*: Innovation and progress in transactions are aimed at improving efficiency, reducing cost, and promoting fairness. A sound transaction environment is of great significance in facilitating economic prosperity and a better life for all. Such innovations include remote transactions, decentralized transactions, and live streaming sales.

How exactly do innovation and technological development influence our national economy? For that, we must first learn to accurately evaluate how advanced a country's economy is. Given that GDP is treated by every economy across the globe as a major index to evaluate their economic activities and growth, we can also probe into how technological development influences GDP and why GDP is limited in reflecting the dynamics of a country's economic activities.

Limitations of GDP Indicators in the Smart and Digital Age

There are severe limitations in using GDP as a major indicator to evaluate economic scale in the new era. The acceleration of scientific and technological progress, the development of new business formats, and the opening of a free model of limitless supply of products have greatly magnified the shortcomings of GDP indicators — there is now an increasing gap between GDP and actual economic activities.

Regardless of their purpose, economic activities are essentially designed to meet social demand and enhance our life quality. Our demands are diversified — the products an economy provides us, including production materials and means of subsistence, are diversified in terms of quantity (scale), quality, and types. Thus, in theory, to measure the level of economic activity we need to evaluate both the quantity and quality of products and services, which is not an easy job.

At present, the universal method of measuring economic scale is to calculate GDP according to certain rules. Under normal circumstances, when we talk about economic growth, we are referring to GDP growth. So, in the era of the new economy, how beneficial is the long-term index of GDP?

According to the final product approach, GDP in a certain period is equal to the sum of expenditure on final products and services. Thus, if the same types of products are produced with different quality, in different times, and sold at different prices, their contribution to GDP is different.

For example, say a country manufactures and sells two types of leather shoes: one pair of regular shoes priced at RMB 500 and the other premium shoes priced at RMB 3,000. In a single statistical year, if a pair of each is produced and sold, then the contribution of the leather shoe industry is equivalent to RMB 3,500.

However, things get more complicated if you consider the inter-period sales and contribution to GDP. Here's a simple example. Say a country produced regular leather shoes in base year t and sold two pairs for RMB 1,000. In the next year, year t+1, it improved the design and technique, stopped producing regular shoes, and started producing and selling premium ones, and again, it sold two pairs but now for RMB 6,000. From year t to t+1, how much did the leather shoe industry contribute to that country's economic growth? Under the current economic calculation system, the improvement in quality cannot be evaluated; however, the price variance — from RMB 500 to RMB 3,000 a pair — is counted as price fluctuation. So, based on constant price, the contribution to GDP in year $t+1$ was still calculated as RMB 1,000 — zero growth; the benefits brought about by improved quality to consumers were completely ignored.

Finally, GDP is measured in terms of the total value of final output. With the rapid development of science and technology, it is common that new products can perfectly replace old ones, and these new technologies, materials, and techniques are both better and cheaper, and produced at a lower cost. But according to the current GDP calculation methodology, their contribution to GDP may be lesser, although they are more high-tech and valuable.

Personal computers used floppy disks with an extremely small capacity to store information in the past, and later turned to not-so-convenient compact discs, and now use portable USB flash drives that have huge storage capacity. Here are some actual numbers. In 1976, Seagate invented the 5.25-inch floppy disks and sold them at USD 390 each, which was quite expensive back then; however, each disk only had 1 MB of storage capacity. In 2020, a typical USB flash drive that can store 32 GB (1 GB = 1,024 MB) costs a couple of dollars only. Therefore, if we still stick to GDP as the evaluation criterion, USB flash drives may well contribute less to the GDP of the IT industry (at least every gigabyte of storage adds less value to GDP), though they have superseded floppy disks.

Short messaging service and WeChat voice messages are much more convenient and cheaper than traditional mails and telegraphs. Also, advances made in medical technology are of critical significance for people to enjoy a better life. Before the founding of the People's Republic of China, it was exceedingly difficult for a patient to seek medical advice and afford medicines, and at times, would spend an entire fortune, and yet be unable to be cured. But now, the same disease may be cured simply by taking some pills or tablets, and even the working class can afford the treatment. Based on constant price, the treatment of pulmonary tuberculosis contributes less to GDP than it did 70 years ago. Some may argue that medical technologies have changed drastically and China's current medical market is larger than it was 70 years ago. It's true. However, if we were to use the medical technologies of the past but enjoy today's level of medical services and achieve today's health and life expectancy, the GDP contributed by the medical industry may be several times or even dozens of times higher.

In addition, in the new economic era, everything is being gradually digitized and connected to the internet, and we are reaching a point of limitless supply of digital products and internet-based services. Due to the large demand-based supply of these limitless supply products, the marginal cost is almost negligible, and the products are sold at extremely low prices or at times for free. For instance, Baidu's search engine, Amap's navigation and location service, and WeChat's social media service and video communication are extremely valuable or even indispensable to some users. But they don't directly charge the users but rather generate profits via advertising and traffic conversion. However, the value of these free products and services is not included in GDP.

Some may argue that GDP is a critical index that assesses output size and economic growth, but in this book, we prefer to see it as the range of economic growth. Using GDP to assess output size and economic growth may seem reasonable in some cases, but it is not flawless or strictly logical. For example, a Xiaomi (a Chinese multinational electronics company) cellphone is worth RMB 3,000 and a Huawei (a Chinese multinational technology company) cellphone is RMB 5,000 — they contribute differently to GDP. Consumers accept and often attribute it to the difference between the two brands in design, settings, quality, and brand influence. Suppose 1 kilogram of rice was sold for RMB 5 last year and the same rice was sold for RMB 6 this year, then people think the price of the rice has increased by 20%. So, based on constant price, the contribution of 1 kilogram of rice to GDP stays the same. If Huawei sold its cellphone launched last year (Mate 7) for RMB 5,000 and the one this year (Mate 8) for RMB 6,000, there would be a 20% price difference. Is this difference, while calculating the GDP growth, counted as an increase in price or an improvement in quality? Rice produced in different years may taste the same, whereas cellphones launched in different years vary significantly. If the difference of RMB 1,000 is taken as "inflation," then why is the quality difference between Huawei and Xiaomi cellphones reflected in GDP, but the difference between Mate 7 and Mate 8 is calculated as negligible in terms of economic growth (based on constant price)?

How Important is Technological Innovation to GDP?

The current GDP calculation system seriously underestimates the positive influence technological innovation has on economic growth, especially quality improvement. Technological innovation not only leads to the creation of new industries and helps expand existing ones but also causes old ones to wither and even collapse due to the subtraction effect. Old products and industries fade away as they are replaced by alternatives that emerge along the tide of technological advancement. But how to include such processes properly and accurately in the GDP calculation system remains a problem.

Science and technology are knowledge-based productivity, bound to transform into material productivity when they are included in the production process. So, technology plays a critical role in modern productivity and has been treated as a primary factor of economic growth for a long time.

Traditionally, technological innovation facilitates economic development via the following two channels:

(1) Technological innovation affects labor force, materials, and objects, increases productivity and promotes economic growth (e.g., the steam engine).
(2) The output value of new industries formed based on technological advancement is a major component of GDP and an important source of economic growth. For instance, cellphones and modern communication services have dramatically changed our lifestyle and communication habits, triggered many emerging industries, and restructured China's national economy.

The above two summaries of traditional economics are too simple and one-sided. Technological innovation brings changes in both quantity and quality, creates new products and industries (addition), and eliminates old ones (subtraction), e.g., digital cameras wiped out film cameras. However, how to quantify the changes in quality and reflect it in GDP and other statistical indexes and how to offset the addition and subtraction effects of technological development to accurately demonstrate changes in economic scale, remain unanswered.

So, to find a proper answer, let's first consider one of the simplest economic models, producing only one homogeneous product — rice. It is a method frequently used in theoretical studies of traditional macroeconomics, to simplify complicated economies as a homogenized product, making them easier for comparison. So, if the GDP of an economy is equal to how much rice it produces in a year, then technological innovation can be analyzed by counting how much more rice is produced per mu

(1 acre = 6.07 mu) because of technology and how much the total rice output increases every year.

However, it becomes much more complicated if we consider two or more products. So, let us assume that an economy originally only produced rice, and later due to technological development, progressed to producing cellphones. Also, to avoid making things too complicated by bringing currency into the picture, we use rice as the unit of measure and the universal equivalent.

In the past, due to inefficient manufacturing techniques, R&D costs that needed to be amortized, and deficient supporting facilities, producing and marketing a cellphone involved relatively high cost — equivalent to selling 20,000 kg of rice. So, if an economy produces 1 million kg of rice and 30 cellphones a year, then the GDP that year is equivalent to 1.6 million kg of rice. Later, with technological advancement, cellphones become better, more cost-efficient, and cheaper. New smartphones gradually replaced old feature phones but were priced much lower than the latter. So, producing 1 smartphone was equivalent to selling 800 kg of rice. If that economy produces 1.2 million kg of rice and 300 smartphones a year, its GDP is only equal to 1.44 million kg of rice — a 10% drop compared to the previous year. It is a huge paradox — there is increased production of both rice and cellphones compared to the previous year, along with an increase in quality, and the actual economic scale has also increased, but somehow, the GDP of the economy has dropped. This is the focal point of this book — the relationship between technological development and GDP.

Many of you would now think about the price issue in GDP, arguing that the GDP or economic growth is calculated based on constant price and that if the cellphones are based on the previous year's price, the GDP this year would be equal to 7.2 million kg of rice, a 350% increase compared to the last year. It is also reasonable in some sense but not strictly logical. First, most economies apply constant price in calculating GDP, to avoid the effect of currency devaluation or inflation. Next, the example does not consider currency issuance and devaluation. Finally, countries, while calculating GDP based on constant price, do not apply the same method to get a result of "7.2 million kg." Here's a practical example. In the early 1970s, the price of computers was much lower than it was previously. But in 1972, high-end HP 3000 computers were sold for USD 95,000 each, roughly equivalent to USD 600,000 in today's terms. Now, China produces and ships over 50 million computers every year, which are, no doubt, much better than HP 3000 in terms of RAM, computing power, and functionality. Based on the price in 1972, China could generate a whopping USD 5 trillion of the output value from computer manufacturing alone if it is counted at the exchange rate of 1972. The number would be even bigger — USD 30 trillion if it is counted at today's exchange rate. However, according to the National Bureau of Statistics, China's GDP in 2019 was around USD 14.4 trillion (current price).

Going back to the example of rice and cellphones, rice produced last year and this year are nearly the same, but cellphones may differ drastically in terms of functionality. According to a consumer survey, most consumers unanimously think that a cellphone is five times more valuable than its counterparts manufactured a year before. Thus, given the difference in quality, GDP this year, based on how we did the math just now, would be 312 million kg of rice (1.2 million + 300 × 5 × 20,000), 18.5 times of the previous year's GDP.

In this case, technological innovation makes it extremely complex to assess economic growth, as the three equations above lead to three distinctive outcomes. The third may seem a little bit reasonable based on how a country's population benefit from the changes. However, countries do the math on current criteria, without considering changes in quality, and thus come up with much smaller GDP numbers. If a country truly sees smartphones as something entirely different from the original feature phones, it will then come to a number close to or even the same as the first result. So, in this age of fast-changing technologies, the current GDP calculation system highly underestimates how much technological innovation contributes to economic growth.

Let's go deeper into the "subtraction effect" of technological innovation with simple models. For that, we need to make some minor modifications. Supposing an economy produces four products — rice, cellphones with voice functions (hereafter referred to as "cellphones"), cameras, and film rolls. In the previous year, it produced 1 million kg of rice, 80 cellphones (10,000 kg of rice for 1 cellphone), 100 cameras (5,000 kg of rice for 1 camera), and 1,000 film rolls (each film roll contains 30 photos and each film roll is equivalent to 10 kg of rice). So, last year, the GDP was equal to 2.31 million kg of rice. This year, the country invented digital photography and integrated the digital lens into its cellphones. Technological innovation increased production efficiency, so it produces 1.2 million cellphones with digital lenses (still equivalent to 10,000 kg of rice for 1 cellphone). You can take pictures and play games on the new cellphones, and each user spends as much as 50 kg of rice on mobile games per year. The photography function totally eliminates the need for cameras and films. Additionally, users can take more photos with their cell phones. Last year, each camera produced 300 photos on average and the whole country took 30,000 photos. But this year, each cellphone produces 1,000 photos on average, and the whole country took 120,000 photos. The rice production volume this year stays at 1 million kg.

Based on a direct comparison, consumers benefit more and the economy has climbed up this year. The production volume of rice remains the same, but more people have cellphones and photography devices, take more photos, and a new mobile game industry has entered the market. All these demonstrate the "addition effect" of technological innovation — as well as the "subtraction effect." Due to the invention and integration of digital technologies, traditional optical cameras and film production are eliminated or replaced; they are rendered obsolete. Despite the "subtraction effect" or "substitution effect," technological innovation generates more benefits for consumers. But the GDP drops a lot based on the current calculation system. In this example, GDP this year is only equal to 2.206 million kg of rice — about 4.5% less than the last year. Here are two pivotal conclusions: First, GDP cannot accurately reflect the economic activities and consumer (people) benefits. Second, technological innovation contributes to the decline of GDP due to the "subtraction effect."

Overall, the example first shows that the current GDP calculation system highly underestimates the positive influence of technological innovation on economic growth, especially on product quality improvement. Second, technological innovation not only creates new industries and helps expand existing ones but also causes old ones to wither and even collapse via the subtraction effect. So, technological innovation sometimes doesn't help GDP climb up but instead pulls it down. Normally, old products and industries fade away as they are replaced by alternatives that emerge along the tide of technological development. But how to precisely demonstrate such a substitution in the GDP calculation system has yet to be addressed.

Influence of Different Types of Technological Innovation on Economy

Influence on GDP varies with different types of technological innovation. Innovation in product function and quality, in new products and services, and in transactions are the most common in the era of the new economy. They make tremendous contributions; however, they are the most likely to be ignored by the current GDP calculation system.

Traditional theories on economic growth and macroeconomy, such as the Solow model and real business cycle model, often treat technological development as a comprehensive, abstract, and homogeneous factor that drives economic growth and fluctuation by influencing production efficiency. This is indeed simple but not sufficient to help us probe into how complex and diversified the influence of technological innovation on the economy is. In the following, we explore how innovations affect economic growth based on how we categorize innovation:

(1) *Innovation that improves means of labor*: Means or materials of labor refer to all those things that transform or influence the object of the labor. The key element is the production tool which determines efficiency. As trucks replace hand-drawn carts, transportation becomes increasingly efficient; as tractors replace cattle for ploughing, agriculture develops better; as machine tools replace manual labor, industrial productivity sees improvement. All these are examples of innovation that improves the means of labor — the most traditional yet common technological innovation aimed at improving production efficiency and thereby creating material wealth and economic growth.
(2) *Innovation that enriches objects of labor*: Objects of labor refer to all the materials to which labor is applied. There are two types: crude materials from nature, such as coal, crude oil, and forests; processed raw materials, such as cotton, steel, flour, and wood. Fiberboard replacing wood and tempered glass replacing steel plates are all examples of innovation in labor objects. As new materials are developed and biological engineering emerges, companies have higher performance and cheaper objects of labor to choose from, which has a significant influence on economic growth. For instance, using engineered plastic instead of certain metals may improve product quality, and make it possible to apply new techniques, such as lamination, spraying, and extrusion, and thus save processing cost; using ceramic materials to produce engines can save a lot of energy and make it unnecessary to apply cooling measures as ceramic is heat-resistant; monocrystalline silicon promotes the rapid development of the electronics industry; using biogenetics to breed

superior farm animals and seeds can prop up both agriculture and animal husbandry.

In general, innovation and diversification in objects of labor greatly increase the number of material products we make, provide consumers with more options, and promote social progress and economic prosperity. But compared with the innovation in means of labor, objects of labor have a more complicated influence on economic growth. Innovation in objects of labor indeed drives productivity forward, such as in choosing the new breed of rice seeds, improving existing ones, and increasing the production volume. Cheap objects of labor generally lead to cheaper products and contribute less to GDP. For example, when making a chair, you can use plastic, metal, fiberboard, or regular wood, or you can choose premium wood, such as *Dalbergia odorifera* and rosewood. Similarly, chairs made from different materials differ in quality, reputation, price, and contribution to GDP.

(3) *Innovation that multiplies product features*: Technological innovations do not just occur in means and objects of labor but also in the improved product performance and quality. It is more obvious in technological products (i.e., medicines and biotechnology products), electronics (i.e., computers and cellphones), and digital products (i.e., software). Take television; from black and white to color TVs, from vacuum tube to crystal valve and integrated circuit, and to the smart and 3D technology, TVs have rapidly improved in performance and quality, just like computers and cellphones. According to Moore's law, when price remains unchanged, the number of components and parts in an integrated circuit doubles every 18 to 24 months, so does its performance. In other words, the computing power that one dollar can buy doubles every 18 to 24 months. But technological innovation centered around product quality doesn't pursue productivity efficiency. There is no standard measure for improvement in quality as it usually doesn't help the manufacturer mark up the products (e.g., better computers are cheaper and more popular). Therefore, the contribution such innovation makes isn't reflected in the current GDP calculation system.

(4) *Invention of new products and services*: Technological innovation also brings forth many new products and services, such as the telephone invented by Alexander Graham Bell, the light bulb by Thomas Alva Edison, and automobiles by Karl Benz. The invention of new products

and services boomed when humans entered the modern age. In the 1940s, the computer was invented; at the end of the 1960s, internet came to the world; in the 1990s, people created e-commerce; and the 21st century is the age of mobile payment. Now, all these inventions are entirely changing our lives and our economic activities.

However, they don't add up, but replace the existing activities. For example, WeChat video chat is replacing the original telephone service, digital audiovisual products are replacing audio recorders and cassette players, cellphone lens is replacing optical cameras and film, and online shopping is replacing in-store shopping. All such disruptive innovations involve existing technologies, products, and services being replaced by new ones, but therein hides the so-called "substitution effect," as we mentioned earlier. According to the current GDP calculation system, the cellphone lens is not able to fill the gap in GDP caused by the disappearance of cameras and film. But it's inappropriate to treat such innovations as futile efforts. It's just that the "substitution effect" is exaggerated while their positive influence on consumer benefits is underestimated.

(5) *Innovation in transaction*: Innovation and popularization of the internet, big data, and smart technologies, and the boom in modern logistics have dramatically facilitated remote transactions, cut out intermediaries, and reduced information asymmetry. Generally, innovations in transactions can not only reduce the cost and expand the scale, which affects GDP in a positive manner, but also greatly reduce intermediaries and reduce commissions, which in turn affects economic growth in a negative manner.

GDP Calculation of Limitless Supply Products

The use value of limitless supply products is not included in GDP if the manufacturer profits from derivatives instead of direct sales. So, their contribution to GDP is greater than what the statistical data show.

Limitless supply has emerged in many industries in the era of the new economy. In fact, intellectual properties derived from scientific research and innovation can be seen as products (factors) of limitless supply. How limitless supply products influence GDP and how to accurately include them into GDP calculation remain a pivotal subject in need of much more attention.

Limited supply products such as bread, steel, and cars, once produced, contribute to GDP irrespective of whether they are sold, as unsold products are counted as inventory assets. But how to check the stock of limitless supply products such as computer software and internet videos and what is the point of doing an inventory check of such products?

We have mentioned this in the previous chapter and delve into the topic deeper in the following chapters — manufacturers of limitless supply products can profit from direct sales (e.g., Microsoft sells its Windows operating system and Office software) and from derivatives by providing products for free (e.g., Tencent's WeChat application can be downloaded and used for free). So, how do different business models influence the GDP calculation system?

With a larger market presence and more users, Microsoft could generate large revenues and make immense contributions to the GDP of the US. It does not need to increase production costs (except for sales and after-sales service) like General Motors or Boeing. For traditional companies making limited supply products, capturing a bigger market entails an increase in cost while contributing more to GDP. Thus, competing for market share is indispensable for such companies.

Like Microsoft's Office, Tencent's WeChat has usage value for all its users. Tencent provides the download and usage of WeChat for free and profits from derivative services. The revenues of course contribute to GDP, but they are in fact generated from other related services of WeChat. As for WeChat itself, the value of social service is because it is free, and it is not included in GDP calculation.

Zero marginal cost and changes brought about by the internet to business models have brought us more free products and services, which have further triggered new industries and brought unmatched convenience to people. Undoubtedly, these free products and services have disrupted and replaced traditional ones with a high output value.

As technology develops, business models shift, and digital and smart economy rises, our lives are experiencing a radical change, which largely outweighs the data reflected in GDP calculation. In other words, in the era of the new economy, contributions of technological innovation and digitalization to GDP are highly underestimated.

Chapter 4

Unique Features of How Limitless Supply Products Generate Profits

Limitless Supply and Long-Tail Theory

As pioneering technologies like the internet and big data get upgraded and become increasingly popular, the number of users that companies have access to are growing exponentially, with transaction costs plummeting and supply becoming limitless. Pinduoduo, WeChat, and Alipay triumphed based on billions of long-tail users.

Limitless supply products, practically speaking, cannot run out — something quite uncommon in the age of traditional economy, but extremely common in the era of digital, smart, and internet-based economy.

For manufacturers, production cost, whether high or low, is fixed, but the marginal cost is zero due to limitless supply. Therefore, for companies, the more the users, the brighter the prospect — "the more, the better." Consequently, marketing stands out as the pivotal element in corporate operation to capture as many users as possible, and marketing expenses take up a pretty large proportion of the total cost.

Users of limitless supply products, on the other hand, could be other companies (e.g., clients of office software), or individuals (e.g., clients of social software and video websites). To companies of such products, if their products and services meet the needs of both large corporations, small- and micro-sized firms, and individual clients, long-tail users are priceless. The 80–20 rule of traditional economics suggests that 80% of your company sales come from 20% of your customers. So, the key to marketing is to serve your key customers well instead of long-tail customers. However, in the era of a new economy, companies with limitless supply products rely on the numerous long-tail users for revenue.

Theoretically, there's a giant gap between the importance of long-tail users and the marginal cost of products. Private airplanes, luxury yachts, and sea view villas cannot cater to long-tail customers. But software, e-commerce, social service, and online games can never depend on a handful of high-end users.

In October 2004, Chris Anderson, *Wired* magazine's Editor-in-Chief, coined the "long-tail" theory to describe the business model of websites, such as Amazon and Netflix. Accordingly, people in the past only cared about people and things of importance. If depicted in a normal distribution curve, the attention falls on the "head," but hardly on the "tail" — people or things that need more energy and cost to throw light on. For example, while selling products, companies care about the few "VIP" users, instead of the most regular customers. But in the internet era, attention costs much less, so companies have an opportunity to cater to the "tail," and the "tail" generates benefits that are even higher than the "head." According to Anderson, in the internet era, we need to focus on the profits made from the "long tail." Given enough shelf space and distribution channels, less popular products that have a low sales volume can collectively make up a market equal to or larger than that of a limited number of popular "hit products."

The long-tail theory is focused on the influence of changes brought about by the internet on business models and transaction methods. All the individualized and less popular products, put together, may exceed a single hit product in scale and sales. For limitless supply products with zero marginal cost, sales revenue equals gross profit, and the user base is a corporate asset — that's why long-tail users are critical.

At present, the worlds' biggest tech giants by brand value, including Facebook, Google, Amazon, Alibaba, Tencent, and ByteDance, which are mostly based in the field of a new economy, enjoy a vast user base, and specialize in limitless supply products and services. Their success is attributable to an enormous user base.

Pinduoduo, a fast-growing e-commerce platform, became the second largest player in China only four years after it was founded, reaching USD 57.7 billion in market value.[1] According to its 2019 annual report,

[1]Closing data on April 24, 2020.

Pinduoduo's gross merchandise volume (GMV) was RMB 1.0066 trillion, annual active buyers were 585.2 million, and full-year revenue was RMB 30.14 billion.

As a typical company that has grown due to long-tail users, Pinduoduo has created multiple highlight features on its homepage, such as daily cash bonus, limited-time flash sale, big brand discount, luxury clearance sale, and bargaining for free, to showcase itself as a low-price platform. Its target audience consists of three groups of people.

The first group is students. They have a low budget but have the desire to buy, so they prefer products that have competitive prices. The second is stay-at-home spouses and young mothers living in second-, third-, and fourth-tier cities. They choose Pinduoduo for its low-price products. The third group is low-income migrant workers and newbies at workplaces. While the platform was in its infancy, it targeted people in small cities and towns who have little or no online shopping experience. In the past couple of years, Pinduoduo managed to attract more users from the first and second-tier cities through word of mouth by means of the "ten-billion-yuan subsidy" program, but those who prefer low-price and low-end products still compose its mainstream customers.

Demand and Pricing of Limitless Supply Products

Limitless supply products cannot be priced using the cost-plus method, as the equilibrium price is not determined by the cost, but by market demand. Casually pricing your products would damage your own benefits, making it extremely hard to maximize profits.

The cost of limitless supply products is based on a complex structure, different from limited supply products. First, they need to invest a large amount of funds in R&D as a sunk cost which doesn't increase with higher production volume. Such a cost structure forms up an enormous economy of scale — the higher the production volume (supply), the lower the average cost.

Cost-plus is the most common pricing method in the traditional economy. But it is of no use to limitless supply products as they have nearly no marginal cost. Some may argue that such products, even without marginal cost, must have a certain average cost. After all, the cake is of limited size, so a product cannot be sold countless times and the average cost cannot be reduced to zero. In this way, products without a large market share should be sold at an extremely high price. But countless copies of Microsoft's Windows operating system have been sold, and Microsoft is still producing its operating system every day. Shouldn't it be free? The fact is quite the opposite.

Scholars think limitless supply products should be priced based on their value,[2] which kind of makes sense because the more valuable a product gets, the higher the price users are willing to pay. However, while pricing an actual product, it's not an easy job to figure out how valuable users think it is. Worse still, users don't have unanimous opinions, so based on whose opinion should we judge the value? If we decide based on the average rating, we are, in fact, ruling out all the users who give a below-average rating. If we decide based on the lowest rating, then many products will hit the price floor, damaging the companies' profits.

Theoretically, limitless supply products have fixed production costs — increasing the production volume doesn't increase the cost. Corporate profit is equal to sales revenue minus the fixed cost. In this case, increasing revenue equals more profits. So, the best price of a product is the price that maximizes sales revenue. Higher costs can increase the per customer transaction cost but decrease the number of users. Lower prices can increase the number of users and sales volume but are not beneficial to increasing profit. So, how do companies strike a balance between sales volume and price?

There is an economics concept called "price elasticity of demand," also known as demand elasticity or price elasticity, meaning that every 1% increase in price leads to several percentage points of decrease in demand (sales). Microeconomics suggests that the higher the price, the more price elasticity of demand. In addition, sales revenue is interlinked with price elasticity. For instance, when price elasticity reaches 1.5, price grows by 1%, while sales drop by 1.5%, and sales revenue consequently drops by around 0.5%.

In this case, if the price goes up by 1%, while sales drop by over 1% — price elasticity is greater than 1, then the price would go up and the sales revenue would reduce. At this point, the price should not be increased but should be decreased. If the price goes up by 1%, while sales drop by less than 1% — price elasticity is less than 1, the increased price generates more sales revenue, which means the price should be increased. When price elasticity stays at 1 (unit elasticity), the price is

[2]E.g., Carl Shapiro and Hal Varian highlighted it in their book *Information Rules: A Strategic Guide to the Network Economy*.

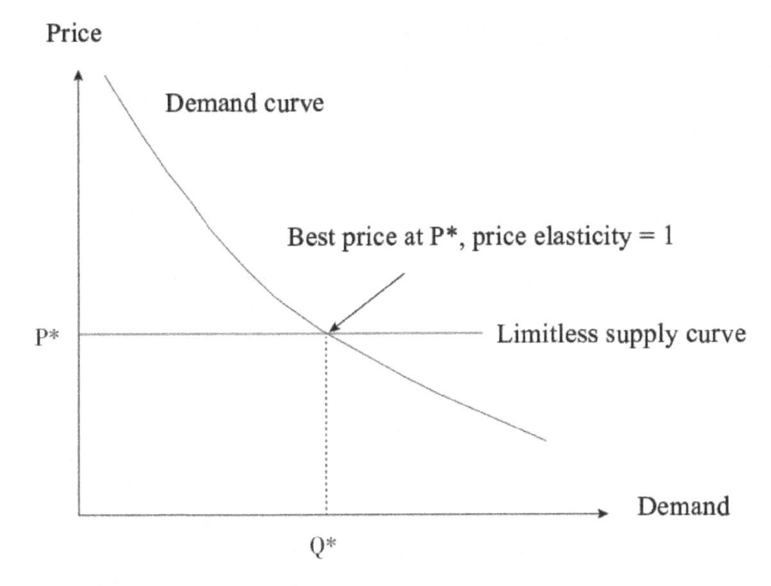

Fig. 1 Equilibrium and best price of limitless supply products.

perfectly balanced, and the sales revenue is maximized (Fig. 1). At this point, the price and sales volume of the product are completely determined by market demand, depicted as a horizontal straight line in terms of supply.

In conclusion, limitless supply products have zero marginal cost, meaning that the manufacturers suffer from no damage even if the products are offered for free. But pricing must be done scientifically and based on actual demand. Casually pricing your products would damage your benefits, making it extremely hard to maximize profits. If enterprises profit from direct sales instead of derivatives, they may sacrifice a handful of users by refusing to lower the price, as their priority is to profit more from richer customers.

For vendors of limitless supply products with zero marginal cost, losing a large number of potential users is always unfortunate. What is ideal is that products are priced soundly and can attract an enormous user base. Vendors of limited supply products also hope to achieve such a goal, and they even have a stronger desire than the former.

For vendors of limited supply products, they have limited capacity and the marginal cost keeps increasing, so profit doesn't scale up with production volume. More importantly, constrained capacity makes it impossible for a single company to capture the whole market. Automobile, real estate, glass, cement, steel, furniture, food, and alcohol markets are all quite large, but none of them is dominated by a single company. But the computer operating system market is literally dominated by Microsoft alone, and nearly all the consumer demands are thus satisfied.

How to both price reasonably and enjoy a large market share (sales volume)? The first answer lies in improving product functionality, quality, and user experience. WeChat, Facebook, Baidu, Toutiao, and other technology companies succeed because they can provide many users with popular services and a good experience. The second is marketing and promoting efficiently, to improve word of mouth and reputation, to increase market demand — shift the demand curve rightwards in microeconomic terms.

Microsoft is known to all as the leading pioneer in the computer operating system field. In the early stage of the PC industry, active suppliers included Apple, International Business Machines Corporation (IBM), and IBM copycats. Apple chose a closed path — customizing its operating system for its own devices only. IBM, due to restrictions of anti-monopoly, had to compete with multiple copycats, so their hardware was rather open-ended. Open hardware led to fierce competition, forcing hardware prices to drop. Due to the bigger price elasticity in the computer market, compatible PCs rose up fast and soon led the market share. So, Microsoft sold its operating system at a low price to other companies, dominating the compatible PC section and the operating system market. Application developers, of course, preferred to work with Microsoft's Windows operating system. Only Apple chooses to develop applications on its own and only for its own operating system. In doing so, developers focusing on Windows competed fiercely with each other, striking a balance in price, gradually improving user experience, and greatly increasing user stickiness. On the surface, it seems like this user stickiness is due to applications, but in fact, it is due to the Windows operating system. Slowly, Microsoft monopolized the PC operating system market, taking up about 90% of the market share. With such a huge advantage, although Microsoft's Windows is quite expensive, it still sells extremely well. At present, a legal copy of Windows 10 in China is worth about RMB 1,000, almost as expensive as a cheap smartphone.

"Honor of Kings" is a mobile game that Tencent launched in 2015. It has been popular for many years now. According to statistics, it had a peak user volume of 200 million players. Due to this huge user base, the game enjoys high user stickiness (especially young players). So, the limitless supply of virtual products in the game, such as tools and character skins, are priced extremely high, from less than RMB 100 to several hundred RMB, enabling Tencent to generate more than RMB 100 million from "Honor of Kings" alone every day.

Price Discrimination — Differential Pricing Strategy

Unlike limited supply products, limitless supply products cannot be graded based on cost differences, however, they can be divided into different versions with different prices based on designated features. Building user profiles using technologies like big data and carrying out a differential pricing strategy based on users' characteristics is of great significance to the sale of limitless supply products.

Limitless supply products have no marginal cost, thus, no matter how cheap they are, so long as they are not sold for free, their vendors are bound to make a profit. If these products are priced too high, many potential customers will not buy or cannot afford the product, hence this would be a waste of user resources. If such products are priced too low, then the vendors may not be able to generate sufficient profit from customers with high purchasing power. So, to overcome this dilemma, enterprises charge differently from different groups of users — a strategy called "differential pricing" or "price discrimination."

That is, an enterprise sells the same product at different prices to different users, or sells slightly different products at different prices even though the cost of producing the differentiated product is the same. According to microeconomics theory, if a supplier segment both users and the market, then they should lower the price of products in markets where there is high demand elasticity and increase the price of products in markets where there is low demand elasticity. In the past, suppliers of limited supply products also carried out the same strategy to sell and profit more. For example, some public parks offer huge discounts on tickets for older people, children, and students; airlines offer higher discounts for passengers who buy tickets a long time in advance; and the international editions of university textbooks published in the USA are sold in developing countries at a much lower price.

Thus, since price discrimination is quite common in limited supply products in the traditional economy, why are we discussing this phenomenon for limitless supply products?

First, for limited supply products such as food items and manufactured goods, a high marginal cost, especially increasing marginal cost and limited capacity, is an insurmountable obstacle during pricing and marketing. For those users for whom the affordable prices are lower than the marginal cost of the product, the use of price discrimination strategies cannot increase corporate profits, and suppliers can only exclude them from effective users. For limitless supply products with zero marginal cost, however, suppliers earn profits easily even if users spend little or no money. Moreover, there is a huge number of long-tail users who are only able or willing to pay a low price, constituting a key source of profit for suppliers of limitless supply products. Therefore, enterprises adopt price discrimination to satisfy the diversified needs of as many users as possible — a significant strategy for suppliers of limitless supply products.

Second, it is relatively easy for limited supply products to achieve market segmentation via product grading. Cars, clothes, food, and real estate can be divided into various grades according to variations in raw material, design, quality, technique, and cost, to satisfy different level users. Take Audi, a famous automaker, for example. Audi manufactures multiple models at the same time — A3, A6, A8, Q5, Q7, and others. Each model has a unique configuration, appearance, performance, and cost, and each model falls into an exclusive grade. Different grades of cars are of course priced differently. High-tier customers with high purchasing power can choose a premium model — Audi A8; mid-tier ones can buy A6 or Q5; regular customers can afford A3. Through product grading, Audi segments both the market and target users, and avoids the traditional sense of price discrimination. However, it is difficult for vendors of limitless supply products to follow this method. Audi produces A6 and A8 models and fundamentally sells them for different prices, as the costs vary significantly, which is not possible for limitless supply products with zero marginal cost. In other words, to grade products by differentiating production costs to target different market segments isn't that easy for vendors of limitless supply products.

Nonetheless, vendors of limitless supply products have come up with possible approaches to make price discrimination work. For instance, once a software is developed, it can be replicated nearly for free and supplied without limit. So, to profit more, software developers often design different versions — professional version and basic version. The professional version is targeted at users with high purchasing power and has high-performance requirements, and the basic version is for so-called low-end users. Some people may think that different versions of an application should be treated as different products, such as Audi A3 and A6, so it is not strictly a practice of price discrimination. However, A3 and A6 are produced at extremely different costs, while the cost of producing the professional and basic versions is nearly at the same marginal cost — zero. Thus, why developers don't provide regular users with something better and stronger? Well, the reason behind that is to achieve differential pricing — maintaining low-end users and while spurring high-end users to pay higher prices.

Vendors of limited supply products try their best to gratify customers with high-quality products and services, to increase sales volume. If it's possible to produce high- and low-end products at the same cost, nearly all enterprises would prefer the former. However, to profit more via price discrimination, vendors of limitless supply products are at times even willing to spend more money to slow down the performance of some products and services. Wolfram Research developed a well-known mathematical software — Mathematica. One day, they launched the student version of the software — they spent the extra money to add a floating-point arithmetic library to the software to eliminate floating-point calculation and slow down the arithmetic and plotting speed, to sell it for a much cheaper price.

Online games contain all sorts of virtual tools, such as rifles and cannons, that cost the same but are sold at different prices, which is also a hidden practice of price discrimination. Some video websites insert ads in videos for non-members while providing ad-free ones for paid members. Non-members can watch the videos, but they must watch the ads as well, which is another manifestation of differential pricing.

Differential pricing must be precise and effective based on user segmentation. In the digital economy, enterprises need to collect enormous information and data about users. Many of them, especially internet companies and big data service providers, can capture all sorts of user data at an extremely low cost, including behavior and habits, income level, payment capacity, hobbies, and consumption features, to construct a precise database of user profiles — the basis for the differential pricing strategy. For instance, enterprises hand out vouchers, online flash sales, and limited-time discounts for customers who have relatively weak purchasing power or are highly price sensitive, to encourage them to obtain loyalty points or cash coupons.

From 1 to N

Multiple functions of a single product generate multiple sources of revenue, which is common in the age of the digital economy and pivotal to limitless supply products. Enterprises can profit from direct sales and other indirect channels or derivatives.

The above discussions on how to price limitless supply products assume that enterprises only profit from direct sales. However, many products such as Alipay, WeChat, and Douyin have exploited multiple earning channels, which is an obvious feature of the new economy era.

The fundamental difference between the limited supply and limitless supply products is not only reflected in supply quantity and marginal cost but in other attributes as well. Limited supply products, including food, cars, and steel, experience loss or depreciation, whereas, limitless supply products do not. A ton of steel, if used to build cars, cannot be used to construct buildings or for the railways. However, an application like WeChat can be used to send text messages, post moments, send red envelopes, transfer money, make payments, conduct video conferences, and even serve as portals of online games and e-commerce activities. A single product can meet diversified needs simultaneously and perform multiple functions, but no matter how you use the product, it does not experience any loss or depreciation.

We call this fact that "1" product meets "N" types of needs "from 1 to N." Of course, some limited supply products have this function as well — you can make phone calls, send or receive messages, download apps, and take and share photos on a mobile phone. But generally speaking, "from 1 to N" is more common in limitless supply products. What's more, suppliers are keen to tap into every possible revenue source from a product that serves multiple functions without much added cost. Therefore, "crossover" operation has become highly fashionable in the digital economy. For example, Tencent is now no longer a company running social platforms and games — it is a news and media corporation, a telecommuting service provider, a financial institution, a smart software developer, a video service supplier, and a mobility service provider. Similarly, Alibaba and its affiliates are not just an e-commerce platform — they are an organization that provides culture, sports, and entertainment facilities, a financial service institution, a cloud service provider, and a big data platform.

"From 1 to N" has generated multiple sources of revenue, which is quite common in the age of the digital economy. For example, video websites can charge membership fees, or charge for certain programs, or sell ads to advertising users, or share sale commissions with live streamers. Tencent, the owner of WeChat, can directly sell its software — charge its users for downloading the software, like what Microsoft does traditionally. However, charging users for the use of its application is just a drop in the bucket compared to the numerous other ways that Tencent can profit and monetize through WeChat. So, how does WeChat, a free chat app, generate huge profits for Tencent?

WeChat enjoys an enormous user base that generates huge traffic, and the traffic, in turn, brings Tencent huge profits. Commissions from operators' traffic fees alone can offset several of Tencent's expenses every day, and such commissions are just the beginning. Every day, we receive notifications from a lot of official WeChat accounts, and each account posts ads. WeChat charges on both opening an official account and posting ads — an ad is charged as much as RMB 0.5 on average. Countless ads bring Tencent a huge amount of revenue per day. Moreover, WeChat hosts many mini-games. Say 10% of its users play these games; that would be about 100 million users. If each user spends RMB 1 on games per day, Tencent can generate a whopping RMB 100 million in revenue. It doesn't end here. WeChat is well-known not only as an instant messaging application but also as a payment platform. WeChat Pay enjoys a huge user base. People buy financial products with the balance in their WeChat wallet, and pay service charges to withdraw funds from their wallet, which is another substantial revenue source for Tencent. More importantly, WeChat attracts innumerable users for Tencent, and Tencent's network empire nearly covers every business in the internet industry in China, including basic life necessities. After downloading third-party apps, we need to sign up using our WeChat account, and these applications must pay a commission to Tencent.

The core product of another internet giant, Baidu, is its search engine. Users can search for news, pictures, knowledge, and product information. A search engine is a typical limitless supply product and service that anyone can use freely without any loss or depreciation to the product. For most ordinary users, Baidu's search service is free, but it doesn't mean

Baidu doesn't profit from it. It generates a huge amount of profit from the following: First, promotion fees from a paid listing. Baidu charges companies based on how many visits they get from potential users. Every day, over 100 million people search for information. Companies bid for search engine optimization (SEO) keywords related to their products into Baidu to make it possible for users to find their websites. Second, Advertising Alliance — from which Baidu gets handsome commissions. Third, advertisements from the Baidu app. Lastly, membership fee for Baidu Music, membership and download fee for Baidu Library, and other value-added services like Baidu Map.

These cases prove that if a product serves multiple functions, suppliers can profit from revenue channels other than direct sales. Furthermore, product developers (suppliers) can use the different functions of the product to diversify their revenue sources.

We call the profits from direct sales "direct yield," and the profits from derivatives "derivative yield." There is a saying popular in the Chinese internet community, "the wool comes out of the dog, while the pig pays for it (the fourth party pays for it)." It is thus clear that derivative yield is of great significance in the new economy, especially in internet-based fields.

Derivative yield also proves the importance of user capitalization. For many enterprises, users are not just consumers but are a "free labor force" that indirectly generates revenues from multiple sources while using their products.

Paid, Free, or Subsidized

For limitless supply products with abundant derivatives and zero marginal cost, being free is not only feasible but also increasingly common. High derivative yield, if possible, allows enterprises to come up with effective subsidy policies and even provide products for free or at a negative price — coupled with subsidies.

How to price a product with derivative yield (indirect revenue)? When to make a product free (no charge)? Is it reasonable to price a product negatively?

As we mentioned earlier, the price of a limitless supply product, if without other sources of revenue, should be balanced at a point on the demand curve where price elasticity equals 1 (unit elastic), thus maximizing the profit. However, such a price, if the product has other sources of revenue besides direct sales, clearly doesn't matter anymore. The reason is simple — as the unit elastic price drops by 1%, the sales volume increases by 1%, offsetting each other in terms of influence on sales revenue (profit). But the increased sales volume also generates higher derivative yield, making the strategy of marking down the product at unit elastic, beneficial. In other words, derivative yield encourages enterprises to mark down their products, to serve more consumers and profit more.

But the problem is, where to place the price on the demand curve when a product generates derivative yield? To put it simply, how to price a product with derivative yield? To find an answer, let us first analyze how marking down the price affects profits. First, an increase in sales volume increases derivative yield. Second, lowering price directly affects (reduces) sales revenue. Undoubtedly, when derivative yield increases more than the decrease in sales revenue, marking down the price of the product is beneficial and should be continued even if the price reaches zero or is a negative number. On the contrary, if things are the other way around, marking down the price would lead to a loss.

Intriguingly, when the demand is represented by a linear demand function (downward sloping line), enterprises are willing to spend half of their derivative yield as subsidies (please refer to the appendix for details). Based on derivative yield, enterprises set positive, zero, or even negative (subsidized) prices for products.

Users are the core resources (assets) of limitless supply product vendors. When users contribute derivative yield to an enterprise, they are not just consumers but should be treated as outsourced workers as well. The notion of negative price is easier to comprehend if we treat subsidies as allowances for users.

In conclusion, for limitless supply products with derivative yield, prices that maximize profits have the following characteristics:

(1) As derivative yield multiplies an enterprise's sources of revenue, the enterprise is willing to mark down products to transfer part of its extraneous income (derivative yield) to users. When demand is elastic (a downward slope), enterprises spend half the derivative yield on marking down the price.
(2) Marking down the price of products isn't the result of excessive profits, but rather, is the first step to attract more users to earn higher derivative yield, which can then be used to cover the decreased sales revenue. The higher the derivative yield, the lower the price, and the

higher the equilibrium quantity. The more sensitive users are to the price, the more effective is the strategy of marking down the price, and the higher the increase in equilibrium quantity.

(3) Derivative yield brings users lower prices, expands the user base, and multiplies the enterprises' sources of revenue. The larger the market presence, the higher the derivative yield from individual users, and the higher the enterprises' profit.

(4) On the demand curve, the best price of limited supply products with positive marginal cost must be at the point where elasticity is greater than 1; for limitless supply products with zero marginal cost, it is at the point of unit elasticity; while for limitless supply products with derivative yield, the price elasticity is less than 1.

(5) When the derivative yield from an individual user reaches a certain threshold, the product is sold for free. When the derivative yield is high enough, the price can even be a negative number. In other words, users can use a product for free, and even obtain rewards or incentives.

Before the internet entered our daily lives, the mainstream business model of the software industry, be it large operating systems or small applications, was charging for usage. From Microsoft to Adobe Systems Incorporated (Adobe), Sun Microsystems, Inc. (SUN) to SAS Institute Inc. (SAS), selling software was their major source of revenue. However, in the internet age, free use became a notion that everyone has taken for granted. From Facebook to Google, Tencent to Baidu, all the mainstream applications can be downloaded for free. While we are still enjoying the daily privilege of free use, the age of subsidy has come, quietly and swiftly — typical ones include Didi (a mobile ride-sharing platform that offers app-based ride-sharing services), Meituan (a Chinese O2O (online-to-offline) local life service platform), and Qutoutiao (meaning "fun headlines" in Chinese, a Chinese mobile content aggregator). The fundamental reason lies in the fact that in the past, Microsoft, Adobe, SAS, and even Kingdee ERP Software in China, could only profit from direct sales. However, in the era of a new economy, everybody has access to the internet, and, therefore, software has become a portal to an enormous user base, and users are a strong positive externality. The two features indicate that software that emerged in the internet age can generate strong derivative yield — the larger the user base, the larger the users' value, and the higher the derivative yield.

It is worth mentioning that in the era of a new economy, enterprises and users usually form a long-term relationship of service and cooperation, and don't just carry out "once-for-all" deals. Enterprises earn derivative yield from their long-term service to users. Though it is common for enterprises to offer subsidies to users, it is, in fact, based on the development stages, as such behavior is usually aimed at attracting customers or competing with one another to quickly grab market share. In addition, enterprises may offer products for free for a long time (e.g., Baidu's search engine, and Tencent's WeChat), but only offer subsidies occasionally. As once users, especially loyal ones, are accustomed to a certain product, they may no longer be triggered by rewards or incentives. Users who are willing to stay loyal only because of long-standing subsidies are mostly not active users or the target users — they are colloquially referred to as the "wool-pulling party (deal hunters)."

Beware of the Deal Hunters

If an enterprise cannot differentiate between target and non-target users, it may end up indiscriminately offering subsidies and rewards, and probably end up attracting the so-called "deal hunters." To avoid loss, enterprises need to be cautious in how and how much they subsidize.

As the free and subsidy models have become a trend, "deal hunters" and "getting the best deals" have also become buzzwords on the internet. Deal hunter is the nickname for people who get the best deals — seek unjust benefits through loopholes in rules. As new industries such as e-commerce, O2O, internet finance, and internet services grow and join the fierce competition, enterprises have implemented large and generous amounts of subsidies and reward plans to grab user resources. "Getting the best deal" has evolved from grabbing free rewards and coupons, into using Peer-to-Peer (P2P) lending platforms, and then into taking advantage of e-commerce platforms. They evolved from individual users into groups, and into professional deal hunters who are well-organized, are in large groups, and have clear labor division. They have even established a complete profit chain. However, deal hunters are never targeting users.

Based on the economic theory of Adverse Selection, if an enterprise cannot differentiate between target and non-target users, it may indiscriminately offer subsidies and rewards, and probably end up attracting the so-called deal hunters. The higher the subsidies, the more active the deal hunters. The reason is that deal hunters are more sensitive and respond much more quickly to the subsidy policies. For target users, subsidies may seem like a small discount, while to deal hunters, any subsidy is rather a generous reward, for them to earn a living.

Therefore, the critical problem for all enterprises is how to allocate subsidies to target users instead of deal hunters? How to make subsidy programs more effective? Providing limitless supply products for free will not cause a financial loss, but subsidizing involves a monetary cost. Without a proper arrangement, subsidy programs may lead to huge financial losses.

Case: Ofo hongbao bikes suffered huge losses caused by deal hunters[3]

In April 2017, to compete with Mobike (a bike-sharing pioneer), its competitor Ofo launched hongbao bikes (bikes marked with cash-filled envelopes), covering more than 70% of its shared bikes. Users placed up to 7 million orders of hongbao bikes per day. Upon placing an order for a hongbao bike, the user could earn RMB 5 on average, and, if lucky enough, could earn up to RMB 5,000. If we only consider the average number — RMB 5 per order, 7 million orders cost a whopping RMB 35 million every day. According to available figures, Ofo earned approximately RMB 10 million at that time, which means it had to bear a net loss of RMB 25 million because of hongbao bikes every day.

At the same time, attracted by this strategy, the deal hunters returned and targeted Ofo, causing it to incur further losses.

Ofo had not installed a Global Position System (GPS) in its bikes, thus it could only manage hongbao bikes on a regional basis, which meant that if any Ofo bike was activated in a designated hongbao region, it would be treated as a hongbao bike.

Furthermore, due to the mechanical locks, users could choose a hongbao region on the Ofo app, enter the registration number of any Ofo bike in that region to get the password and unlock the bike without scanning the QR Code. As soon as the bike was unlocked, the user could turn on the "ride" mode, ride the bike for 10 minutes, park it anywhere, lock the

---

[3] *Source*: *Didi and other investors weep at the flaws in Ofo hongbao bikes that may cause RMB 25 million per day*, sohu.com, www.sohu.com/a/136057371_451173 and other public materials.

bike and earn the cash reward. Soon, people uploaded and shared instructions on how to exploit the flaws of hongbao bikes — a list of Ofo bike registration numbers (was already viral on the internet), how to root or jailbreak the mobile phone (gain privileged control, known as root access, over Android or iOS systems) to install fake GPS software, upgrade the Ofo app, set the mobile phone's location in a hongbao region, open the app, click "start riding," and manually enter a bike registration number. After that, the app starts timing and charging and the system is notified that the bike is a hongbao bike. Then, the user waits for 10 minutes, sets the location as 500 meters away, clicks "stop riding," and claims the money.

Someone did the math — each user earns RMB 5 every time he/she "rides" a hongbao bike (a single user can order no more than 16 bikes per day), so he/she can earn about RMB 90 per day. If a user opens 20 accounts, he/she could earn up to RMB 1,800 per day and earn over RMB 50,000 in a month. This flawed strategy didn't bring Ofo real users, but only ended up feeding the "wool-pulling deal hunters."

In terms of economics, to alleviate the loss caused by deal hunters, enterprises should adhere to the following principles when implementing subsidy programs:

(1) Pay attention to new users' contribution margins (added derivative yield or value) and allocate subsidies in a rational manner. Enterprises must clarify the average derivative yield or value that new users contribute, and subsidies should be, if there is no special reason, significantly lower than the average added derivative yield, in principle.
(2) Carefully and reasonably lay down subsidy rules, and alleviate losses caused by deal-hunters through technological means.
(3) Implement targeted subsidy programs by analyzing customers' behavior, habits, and price sensitivity using big data. Enterprises should allocate subsidies to valued users, instead of indiscriminatingly offering subsidies.

Here are some strategies enterprises can refer on how to avoid deal hunters:

(1) Clarify the purpose, target users, and estimated results of the subsidy program; figure out the cost and benefit of the subsidy program; and make every cent count.

(2) Test before launch. A thorough security test must be conducted before launching a marketing campaign — to become familiar with all the procedures and spot any potential flaw. During the test, enterprises must try to find loopholes in network security, and repeatedly verify the business logic, to avoid any marketing leak that could be exploited by deal hunters.
(3) Lift the threshold. Awards or incentives should be given to new users after they complete filling up their personal information instead of right after registration. Enterprises should set different thresholds for different scenarios. For instance, in the case of investment and wealth management applications, after registration, the users should be asked to fill in their real names or invest in a certain amount of money, before they can earn any reward. It makes the behavior of "getting the best deals" much harder. What is more, facial recognition can be added as a part of the registration process, to effectively avoid deal hunters.
(4) Setting threshold for registration. Marketing to attract more users increases registrations. But the short-term rapid increase in registration may lead to the danger of multiple deal hunters. So, enterprises, especially their technical teams, must pay close attention to any abnormal changes in registration, and adjust strategies in time.
(5) Identify users' mobile phone numbers. After the users complete the registration, enterprises can identify users' mobile phone numbers based on multiple sources such as network status, traffic, and location, and mark and block any abnormal number.
(6) Ensure flexibility of subsidy and promotion campaigns and tightly control them. Enterprises should ensure they hold the right to, if necessary, abort promotion campaigns and adjust subsidy programs in accordance with the law. Enterprises need to pay close attention to the traffic data of their subsidy programs. In case of any major anomaly, enterprises must, while maintaining a good image, take remedial measures.

Integration of Limitless and Limited Supply

In many cases, to reach users, limitless supply products need to be combined with supporting limited supply products. Whether to sell limitless supply products alone or integrate them with supporting limited supply products into final products is a difficult decision.

In the field of a new economy, many limitless supply products need to be combined with limited supply products before they finally reach the customers. For example, the facial recognition system needs to be integrated with hardware like cameras; automatic driving technology needs to be applied to vehicles; operating systems need to be installed on computers or mobile phones; smart service robots need to have software, algorithms, a body, and arms and legs. Despite all this, an enterprise can still choose to only sell limitless supply products, and ask users to purchase supporting products, or, it can choose to sell both limitless supply and limited supply products in a bundle.

Two technology behemoths of the modern world, Microsoft and Apple, both produce and sell limitless supply products, such as operating systems and supporting software. However, they differ greatly in product R&D and marketing strategies. Specifically, Microsoft focuses on developing software, then authorizes its dealers to sell its software to computer vendors and users. Whereas Apple chooses to integrate operating systems and hardware — combining its core software (limitless supply) with its own hardware (limited supply) into a final product and launch it in the market.

The above two sales models have their unique advantages and disadvantages and enjoy popularity among a large population. For instance, most film and television companies use the direct sales model like Microsoft, selling content to chain cinemas or TV stations; they seldom build theaters or TV stations themselves. Whereas Bubugao learning machine and Tesla self-driving cars choose Apple's strategy of integrating software and hardware.

When mutually complementary limitless supply and limited supply products are combined, the former further intensifies the functions and use-value of the latter. Here are some practical examples. Without Apple's operating system, the iMac and MacBook (Apple computers) would not be that useful or valuable to users. Tesla cars installed with Tesla's self-driving technology, make driving more convenient. Hence, most customers are willing to pay extra for integrated final products — a higher price than both limitless supply and limited supply products that are sold individually.

Joint R&D and sales of limited supply and limitless supply products can guarantee higher compatibility and neutralize the technological bottleneck of the former (usually hardware) or the limited market access. The disadvantages, on the other hand, are that the market doesn't easily accept limitless supply products, thereby reducing the sales volume. Now, we have mentioned the case of Apple several times. Although it is one of the greatest technology corporations across the world, Apple is still the runner-up in terms of the operating system. Apple's Mac OS is way behind Microsoft's Windows in market share of universal computer software, and Apple's iOS can't catch up with Google's Android in the smartphone market. The fundamental reason lies in Apple's strategy of integrating its operating systems with hardware instead of selling software alone. Of course, there is nothing wrong with it, as the hardware alone has brought Apple enormous profits.

An enterprise that specializes in the R&D of limitless supply products, if it wants to integrate both limitless supply and supporting limited supply products as a bundle, needs to have the following qualifications. First, the limitless supply products must be at the center of the business, such as provide a critical or indispensable influence or it should be of great value on its own, such that it is worth combining with supporting equipment. Second, a bundle can play a greater role than if the products were considered individually — like "1 + 1 > 2"; the final products, once integrated with the limited supply products, are popular enough across the whole market, and generate enough extra profits that offset the possible loss caused by the decreased sale of limited supply products. Third, the enterprise must be equipped with sufficient capital and technological strength to manufacture limitless supply and supporting limited supply products concurrently.[4]

---

[4]If a limited supply product can be universally applied or equipped with mature technologies, then production outsourcing is also an option.

Chapter 5

How Enterprises Grow with Limitless Supply

Review of Traditional Enterprise Growth Models

The analysis of enterprise scale in traditional economics is essentially the theory of capacity determination, and the focus is on the supply side. Enterprises rely on land, capital, labor force, and other factors to grow.

Enterprise growth, like human growth, is a process that moves from quantitative growth to qualitative growth. To be more specific, there is growth in enterprise scale, improvement in internal structure, and enhancement of functionality. Enterprise growth consists of several stages or lifecycles — entrepreneurship stage, expansion stage, maturity stage, and ageing stage.

To highlight how limitless supply and limited supply product vendors differ in terms of growth, we have focused on production scale. The growth or enterprise growth described in this chapter, if not specified, refers to the growth in production scale.

In traditional microeconomics, a production function is used to describe production scale or productivity Q. The production function refers to the input–output relationship on a certain technological basis. If A represents technological level, K represents capital, and L represents labor, the function is

$$Q = A \cdot f(K, L).$$

In other words, production scale is determined by technological and input levels. At a relatively stable technological level, enterprise growth depends on increased input. That is, input determines capacity, while capacity determines the maximum productivity. So, how fast an enterprise grows depends on how quickly its capacity expands. In the short term, K is fixed input that can't be changed, while L is flexible input that can be adjusted swiftly. Therefore, companies can modify input of labor force according to demand to adjust output scale. In the long run, changing the scale of capital input is much more pivotal in adjusting capacity.

So, how traditional economics analyze company scale boils down to capacity, with focus on the supply side. Demand affects scale by stimulating the company's input intention. A strong demand causes companies to increase input and expand capacity, whereas a weak demand leads to an opposite result. Without expanded capacity, demand alone, no matter how strong, cannot help to expand the scale.

It is clear from the production function that the growth rate of output is determined jointly by technological progress, capital stock, and workforce size. Production functions, especially the Cobb–Douglas production function, indicate that there is a certain substitution between capital and labor. However, from the perspective of cost optimization and balanced factor allocation, there should be a reasonable proportion of capital and labor. Therefore, large enterprises in the traditional economy, whether they be steel companies, automobile manufacturers, textile factories, or chemical enterprises, all have "three highs" — high revenues, high total assets, and high number of employees. Thus, fast growth usually depends on increasing the capital scale and workforce.

Production functions in microeconomics have been extensively applied to macroeconomics analysis and economic growth theories. The neoclassic economic growth model usually treats all output factors as product output. The annual total output represents a country's general income level, while the total output itself is jointly determined by technological level (production efficiency), capital stock, and workforce size.

How Do Vendors of Limitless Supply Products Grow?

Growth of limitless supply product vendors does not depend on capacity expansion but rather on developing a larger user base. Thus, what determines a company's scale and growth rate has entirely shifted from the supply side to the demand side.

When a product reaches the stage of limitless supply and replication, then the traditional production function and the input–output relationship described by this type of production function, the growth of the enterprise, and the law of economic growth are completely meaningless, as any such product, once produced, can be replicated countless times quickly at nearly zero cost. Thus, the supply side is no longer a constraint for enterprise growth. What determines enterprise's growth scale and rate has entirely shifted to the demand side. In other words, enterprise growth does not depend on capacity expansion anymore but rather depends on a larger user base, which has completely disrupted traditional economics theory. Of course, this is not to say that the supply side has become insignificant and that the demand side has become extremely strong. To a certain extent, it depends on whether the enterprise can develop one or multiple products with superior performance and sufficient attractiveness to users that have strong performance and can attract users.

The main basis for distinguishing software companies, internet companies, big data service companies, and large companies from small companies is the number of customers and the value of their per capita contribution. Microsoft is much more well known than Standard Software in China (they are both operating system providers) and has higher market value and sales volume. The fundamental reason behind this is the user base — the former enjoys around 4 billion users, while the latter only has 50 million users. Facebook and WeChat nearly dominate the world's social network market, as they both have an enormous user base.

Since user base (contributed value per capita) is key to enterprise scale and value, every business entity, especially vendors of limitless supply products, strongly desire to quickly gain more users and increase their sales revenue (including derivative yield). The question is, how do they go about it. The following are some of the ways companies attract users:

(1) Guarantee product quality, performance, price–performance ratio, and user friendliness — this is basic business common sense.
(2) Understand your target customers. A critical step to create user profiles is understanding users' interests, needs, ages, professions, and social status. Once there is sufficient information, it is much easier to

figure out what users are interested in and what are the problems they are facing, and it is easier to provide them their favorite products accordingly, thereby earning their trust.

(3) Apply sound promotion and advertisement strategies. In the internet age, enterprises have multiple channels and methods to promote their products. In addition to advertisements, social platforms, video websites, and paid traffic are all major methods to strengthen brands and attract more users. Traditional companies prefer to invest money in equipment and raw materials, while vendors of limitless supply products prefer to invest in R&D and promotion.

(4) Word-of-mouth (WOM) marketing or spontaneous marketing effect. Loyal users can recommend products to friends, colleagues, and online friends, and the word of mouth can spread rapidly. In this way, new users can grow exponentially. WOM marketing is extremely useful in early and middle stages of promotion.

(5) Exploring new channels to expand derivative yield. Any product, no matter how big its target market and how many potential users there are, eventually reaches a saturation stage, thus it can no longer grow without limitations. For example, Facebook has about 3 billion users now and Tencent has 1 billion — there may be no room for expanding the user base. So, to keep growing and branching out, such companies need to explore new domains, develop new products, or add new functions to existing ones to find more channels to generate derivative yield. The history of WeChat is the best example.

Case: WeChat's development and customer growth history[1]

WeChat is a free instant-messaging app for smartphones launched by Tencent on January 21, 2011 and initiated by the R&D team led by Allen Zhang (Zhang Xiaolong). WeChat users can share voice, video, picture, and text messages for free (excluding data fees charged by the network provider) with other users on different networks and even using different operating systems. There are several other functions in WeChat, such as

[1]*Source*: WeChat history. https://zhidao.baidu.com/question/149721893-2069201699.html and other public materials.

sharing of location, social functions such as "Moments," "Official Accounts," "People Nearby," etc.

On January 21, 2011, WeChat (Weixin in Chinese) released the v1.0 beta for iPhone users. WeChat version 1.0 only supported importing existing contact information through a QQ account and only provided simple functions, such as instant messaging, sharing photos, and changing profile photos. In the beta versions 1.1, 1.2, and 1.3, WeChat added functions such as reading mobile phone contact list, linking with Tencent Weibo's private messages, and multi-people conversation. As of the end of April 2011, WeChat had had 4–5 million registered users.

On May 10, 2011, Walkie Talkie released version 2.0, adding Live Voice chat functions, such as Walkie Talkie, and saw a significant growth in user base for the first time.

In August 2011, WeChat launched "Finding People Nearby," and the number of users reached 15 million. As of the end of 2011, the number had surpassed 50 million.

In March 2012, WeChat had over 100 million users. On April 19, 2012, WeChat 4.0 was released, with a new gallery function like that of Path (a private social application on Facebook) and Instagram (photo and video feed), so that users could share their photos to Moments.

In April 2012, Tencent renamed the overseas version of WeChat 4.0 as "WeChat" and decided to embark on the road of international expansion and added multiple language options.

On July 19, 2012, WeChat 4.2 was integrated with video chat applets, and the WeChat website was released.

On September 17, 2012, the WeChat team announced that registered users had surpassed 200 million.

Late on the night of January 15, 2013, the number of users exceeded 300 million, making WeChat one of the communication software with the most downloads and largest user base in the world.

On February 5, 2013, WeChat 4.5 was released, which supported real-time talkback and multi-people real-time voice chat. It upgraded the "Shake" and QR-code functions and supported search, save, and transfer of chat history. What is more, users could receive voice notifications and navigate using locations sent by friends.

In August 2013, WeChat 5.0 was released with new features, such as emoji store, game center, and upgraded Scan (313 in short) — users could scan street views, bar codes, QR codes, words for translation, and covers.

On August 15, 2013, WeChat International exceeded 100 million registered users and registered nearly 30 million users within a month.

On October 19, 2013, WeChat LBS (location-based service) graphic and text reply was launched. Shop owners could register the location of their shops, and when users shared their locations, they could find the nearest shops and use "one-touch navigation" or "one-touch dial" to reach the shops. Furthermore, special offers (e.g., coupons and scratch cards) from the selected shop would be shown on the screen.

On October 24, 2013, WeChat's user base surpassed 600 million, with daily active users (DAU) reaching 100 million.

On January 4, 2014, WeChat integrated "Didi Dache" (Didi car hailing).

In March 2014, WeChat officially launched WeChat Pay.

On August 28, 2014, WeChat Pay announced "WeChat Smart Life," an industry-wide solution. Based on "WeChat official account + WeChat Pay," WeChat planned to transfer traditional business models onto the WeChat platform.

The closed-loop mobile internet solution that WeChat offered contained mobile e-commerce portal, user recognition, data analysis, payment settlement, customer relationship maintenance, after-sales service, rights protection, and social platform advertising. WeChat strode ahead into the commercial circle, connected with partners, and upgraded traditional business models to mobile-internet-based models.

By helping partners "connect everything," WeChat was reshaping people's "smart" life. WeChat integrated services, such as car hailing, electricity bill payments, shopping, medical services, and hotel booking, into its application and provided standard solutions for dozens of traditional industries, including medical services, hotels, retail stores, department stores, restaurants, ticket services, and express services.

On January 21, 2015, WeChat launched version 6.1 on the App Store (Apple's application store). WeChat 6.1 added three major features — red envelopes as attachments, saving of custom emojis if users change mobile phones, and searching content in Moments and nearby restaurants.

Since March 1, 2016, WeChat Pay has stopped charging commissions for transfers but started doing so for withdrawals.

At midnight of January 9, 2017, the much-anticipated mini programs were first launched in WeChat. Users could access services from a variety of mini programs.

On May 4, 2017, WeChat Pay worked with CITCON to enter the US market. Since then, people living in and traveling to the US can enjoy convenient cash-free payment and pay for nearly anything in RMB via WeChat Pay.

On December 28, 2017, WeChat 6.6.1 added in-app mini games and recommended the game "Jump" on the home page.

In February 2018, WeChat's global monthly active users exceeded 1 billion.

In October 2019, WeChat launched "transfer by mobile number," so that strangers could directly transfer money to a user's WeChat Balance.

If you look at the chronology, in the first three months of its launch, WeChat got about 5 million users. This number went up to 100 million within less than a year and up to 300 million in another year. WeChat experienced explosive growth, and even the best traditional companies cannot expect such an explosive growth rate. This is the beauty of limitless supply products and how they differ from limited supply products. For the latter, no matter how strong the market demand is, capacity must be expanded in an orderly manner, with huge input of material and human resources; whereas for the former, without capacity constraints, they can quickly satisfy massive demand, and enjoy fission-type growth.

Viral Marketing and Enterprise Growth

If limitless supply product vendors can quickly attract customers via viral marketing and provide good follow-up services, then they will inevitably experience fission-type growth.

Viral marketing is a business strategy that uses existing social networks to attract users or promote a brand. As its name suggests, consumers spread information about a product to other people, much in the same way that a virus spreads from one person or computer to another. Viral marketing starts from the information source and snowballs and spreads via WOM. Economists refer to this information transmission strategy as viral marketing because it enables marketing information to spread like a virus to millions of people.

The effectiveness of viral marketing mainly depends on the following factors: (1) initial point; (2) infectivity; (3) infection path and media, and measures to strengthen infectivity; (4) infection conversion or implementation.

Any virus starts from an initial point. If the virus originated in a sparsely populated island, it can't spread quickly across the country or even the world. Therefore, the initial marketing planning must be exceptional when it comes to choosing the suitable time, location, and method, and must find topics that both suit the preference of target customers and help promote the product positively in a bid to become a blockbuster.

For example, Jiangxiaobai, a Chinese light-aroma baijiu (liquor) brand that produces grain spirits and focuses on the young adult market, tastes like entry-level liquors; however, it became viral in China. What gave this brand the enormous traffic it achieved and what is behind its popularity? Its advertising copywriting is filled with words that touch people's emotions — it encourages the target customers, makes them feel warmth within, and is intoxicating. Baijiu, or Chinese liquor, has always been an emotional product. Most of the time when people are drinking baijiu, it's not the alcohol that they enjoy all that much but rather the atmosphere and the emotions that the alcohol triggers. Put simply, Jiangxiaobai went viral not because of its quality but due to its market positioning and advertising that enabled it to spread and touch customers' hearts, so that customers were willing to share this brand with others and help promote it. If sharing certain content can enhance your value in the eyes of others or help you release your own emotions, you will be willing to help share and spread.

Marketing information must be simplified to make it easy to spread through WeChat, Weibo, small videos, and other self-media — the shorter the better, and the deeper the impression it gives, the better it is. Companies can employ several methods to accelerate the process, such as rewarding both the recommenders and those who have received the recommendation. Double the rewards could double the efforts and even lead to tenfold results.

Dissemination is indeed critical, but it won't work if the person to whom the information is spread is immune to information — even though many people know the product, very few would like to pay. Therefore, increasing user conversion rate — turning "infected" people into active users and new "virus carriers" — is key. To do this, companies need quality products and valuable services. Product design in the digital era is centered around "touching consumers' heart" or reflecting the nature of the industry because fundamentally, no one can keep selling inferior-quality products for long. Moreover, due to the strong polarization brought by the internet, competition is even more fierce. Even if you are 1% stronger than your competitors in some way, a good word-of-mouth campaign may amplify this by 100%, resulting in large sales growth.

If limitless supply product vendors can quickly attract customers via viral marketing and provide good follow-up services, then they will inevitably experience fission-type growth. Jiangxiaobai is exceptionally good in its marketing; however, each bottle of liquor is produced at some cost, which means that sales volume is still limited by capacity. But this is not the case for limitless supply products like Douyin and Alipay, as having a large user base alone can generate revenues. So, for them, the first step towards growth is attracting users.

User Growth Patterns of Limitless Supply Products

User growth is the key driving force for vendors of limitless supply products to grow and branch out. In this case, user growth is divided into the following five stages: initial stage (I), explosive growth stage (II), slow growth stage (III), plateau stage or saturation stage (IV), and decline stage (V).

As we mentioned earlier, user growth is the key driving force for vendors of limitless supply products to grow and branch out. Compared with traditional enterprises, vendors of limitless supply products have a much faster rate of growth. As a company that offers news and consulting service, how did Toutiao surpass the first generation of internet companies like Sina and Sohu in such a short time? As e-commerce platforms, how did Alibaba, Pinduoduo, and JD.com grow so fast while Dangdang (a Chinese electronic commerce company) is on the decline? Let's briefly look at and analyze the key factors (parameters) affecting the growth of limitless supply products, to help answer the above questions:

(1) *Promotion and advertising intensity*: This indicator can be assessed as a unit of time, for example, the total number of people who have viewed the advertisement within a month or a year. Advertising is a key component of corporate management and nearly as critical as product R&D for vendors of limitless supply products. In general, the more intense the advertising campaign, the more customers the enterprise can attract.

(2) *Promotion conversion rate*: This pivotal indicator refers to the ratio of people, who have seen or have been targeted by the promotion, being converted into users. It can be affected by many factors, such as target customers, product usage and quality, competitiveness, price–performance ratio, and promotion methods. In addition, promotion accuracy is also vital. If promotion doesn't work on the target customers, the conversion rate would be pretty low. In the internet age, there is a phrase people mention frequently — precision marketing. It means to precisely aim promotion and advertising at your target customers to increase conversion rate.
(3) *The rate of WOM spread or spontaneous marketing*: Spontaneous marketing is a powerful tool for companies to attract users and branch out. It refers to users or fans spreading the product information spontaneously, as they willingly recommend products to their friends, families, and other online friends. It is a key prerequisite for viral marketing. With spontaneous marketing, enterprises need to spend little to trigger the viral effect to attract new users. Spontaneous marketing is closely related to externalities such as popularity (WOM). Usually, customers only recommend a certain product if they really like it. However, social platforms such as WeChat and Weibo have strong externalities. The more users they have, the more valuable and stronger they are in spontaneous marketing.
(4) *Churn rate*: For any enterprise or product, losing old customers has become a norm. For example, users of China Mobile Communications (CMCC) switching to China Telecom, Apple users switching to Huawei, Weibo users canceling their accounts, etc. The churn rate, also known as attrition rate, plays a vital role in a company's growth and user base and may be affected by changes in market structure, consumption habits, and competition with substitutes. When people mention "improving customer stickiness," they are talking about reducing the churn rate.
(5) *Market size (total quantity of potential users)*: Each product is targeted at a certain group of people. Products with different features may have entirely different target customers. For example, mobile phone users account for about 80% of the population, while hearing aids are sold to people with hearing loss. In short, the size of the target customers is the number of users based on the limiting conditions. A product with a small group of target users has relatively slow user

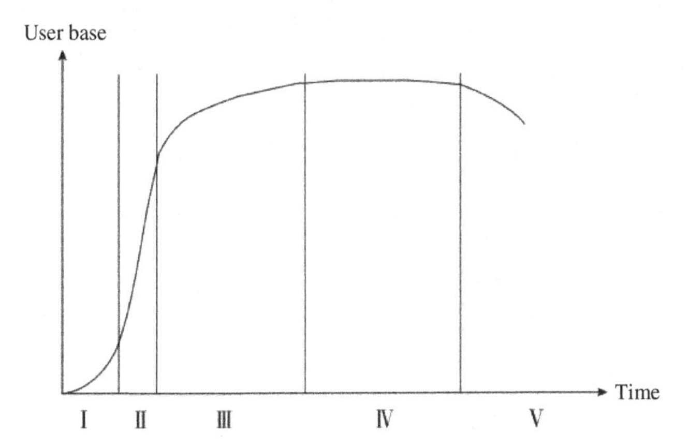

Fig. 1 Growth cycle of limitless supply product user base.

base growth, and its high-speed growth period lasts for a short time. Sudden and explosive growth occurs more easily for products with a large user base, such as WeChat and Douyin.

So, given the influence of the above parameters, user growth of limitless supply products can be divided into the following five stages: initial stage (I), explosive growth stage (II), slow growth stage (III), plateau stage or saturation stage (IV), and decline stage (V) (see Fig. 1).

Initial stage: In this stage, a product's users and fans are few, thus there are not many people helping spread it via WOM. So, to attract new users, the company must focus on promotion and advertising. Even with all promotion efforts, the user base will not grow that fast; however, the growth rate would be big due to the small base number — may be a 100-times growth from 100 to 10,000 people.

Explosive growth stage: After a period of extensive promotion, a product would have accumulated some users, and now a group of loyal users could volunteer to be the "voluntary marketing staff," giving full play to the spontaneous marketing effect. Users are a powerful resource if they volunteer to recommend the products in their social circle. However, there are still a lot of potential targeted users that are yet to be reached. There is still a long way to go in marketing. When a user's friends are not yet familiar with or haven't used a certain product, the user could recommend it to them, which is one of the best ways to attract more users in this stage. Of course, not all limitless supply products can have the chance to experience explosive growth. Many fail before reaching that stage. The engines for an enterprise's explosive growth are optimal opportunity and an initial point.

Slow growth stage: While the explosive growth lasts for some time, the product's user base would soon near the total number of target users. Now, the user base is still growing but at a much slower pace. Promotion efforts now, instead of focusing on bringing new users, is rather aimed at enhancing brand influence. It's like fishing in a river. When there aren't that many fish left, even with the best fishing gear, you won't catch many fish. In the same way, spontaneous marketing won't work that well. If a user is surrounded by friends who are familiar with the product, no matter how hard the user tries, not many people would be attracted to join the fan group. Take WeChat as an example. When the user base reached about 1 billion, no matter how hard it tried and how excellent the WOM was, WeChat could never again experience the surge it did during 2012–2014 in China.

Plateau and decline stage: When a product's user base reaches the total number of target users, the growth rate comes to a halt, entering the plateau stage or saturation stage. There is no fixed duration for the plateau stage, but it always ends because of substitute goods, which take away its users, pushing the product to the decline stage. This is quite common in online games. Once a game hits the peak player base, a new game shows up and takes away the players. With fewer and fewer players, the game gradually declines and is eliminated. Sina and Sohu once dominated the Chinese market — they served as key sources of news and information and enjoyed an enormous user base. Several years later, these old web portals are dwarfed by new players like Toutiao in terms of active user number, views, and advertising revenue. So, when a product reaches the plateau stage, new products and services must be developed, or new channels of derivative yield must be explored, for the enterprise to continue marching ahead.

Table 1 Zoom's profit model.

Basic Personal Meeting Free	Pro Great for Small Teams USD 14.99/Month/Host	Business Small & Med Business USD 19.99/Month/Host Starting at 10 Hosts	Enterprise Large Enterprise-Ready USD 19.99/Month/host Starting at 50 Hosts
Sign Up, It's Free	Buy Now	Sign Up, It's Free	Contact Sales
Host up to 100 participants	All features included in Basic+	All features included in Basic+	All features include in Enterprise+
Unlimited one-on-one meetings	Host up to 100 participants	Host up to 300 participants	Host up to 1,000 participants
Group meetings for up to 40 minutes	Increase participants	Increase participants	Unlimited cloud storage
Unlimited meetings	Meetings for up to 24 hours	Telephone support	Customer success manager
Online support	User management	Control panel	Administrative business audit
	Administrator features	Real-name website	Discounts for buying online seminar + Zoom Rooms
+Video conferencing	Reports	Local deployment options	
+Group meeting	Customize personal meeting ID	Managed domain	
+Group writing	Implement schedules and arrange personnel	Single Sign On	
+Security	1GB MP4 or M4A Cloud recording	Corporate brand	
	Skype for Business (Lync)	Customized e-mail address	
	+Optional add-ons	LTI integration	
		Cloud recording transcript	
		+Optional add-ons	

Source: Official website and prospectus of Zoom.

Case: History and success of zoom[2]

Zoom's business and profit model

Zoom is a cloud-based video conferencing solution that works directly in internet browsers. It was founded in 2011 by Eric Yuan in Silicon Valley. Eric Yuan is Chinese and had previously worked at Cisco as a major programmer of Webex, Cisco's video conferencing application.

Zoom currently operates seven products — mobile device, desktop, laptop, conventional video conferencing system, voice message, chat, and file sharing — and can support tens of thousands of people attending a single video conference.

Zoom generates revenue from a free + added-value model (Table 1) — the free version for individuals and small users and the paid versions (professional version and enterprise version) for clients who need more customized features. The free version supports 40 minutes of video conference each time (a notice pops up at the 35th minute stating that the video conference will be disconnected in 5 minutes; paid members don't have time restrictions).

The paid versions are charged either by the number of attendees or by month. From the perspective of obtaining or retaining users, the entire profit model depends on the key role played by the conference host. The host is the person who sends the conferencing invitation and decides to use Zoom to convene a meeting. So, the host is mostly the individual user who has paid for the membership.

The behavior of the meeting host is the main indicator of profitability, and different payment models are determined by the different roles of the host. Zoom's payment model is also based on the host's role, number of participants, and number of hosts (related to size of the company for enterprise accounts). Each host account costs USD 14.99–19.99. According to the information disclosed in Zoom's April 2019 prospectus, Zoom had about 50,000 enterprise users at the time of which 344 enterprise users paid more than USD 100,000 per year.

---

[2]*Source*: Public materials from "qqchanpin," "Zhouzuoluo (ID: fangdushe007)," "36Kr," "Tiger Brokers," and sina.com.cn.

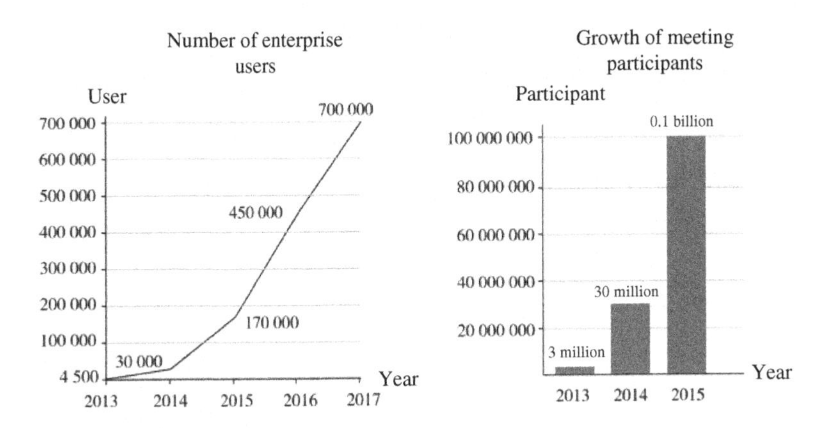

Fig. 2 Zoom's rapid growth trajectory.

Source: Qqchanpin (author: Shirley): Racking up over half of Baidu's market value in a month after going public; how did Zoom nail product growth? https://new.qq.com/omn/20190519/2019051-9A01M06.html?pgv_ref=aio2015&ptlan=2052.

Zoom's rapid growth trajectory

Zoom's goal is to develop a product that directly competes against Webex. It is by no means a new product or a market; it is rather a red sea filled with leading enterprises. Besides Webex, there are many other major players, such as Skype, Google Hangouts, Adobe, Citrix, along with minor ones, such as BlueJeans, GoToMeeting, Highfive, and Join.Me.[3]

Zoom has not only survived in the fierce videoconferencing market, but it has in fact prospered and achieved rapid growth. According to Fig. 2, Zoom has an outstanding growth curve, matching the track of initial stage and explosive growth stage. The reason Zoom could stand out among all its competitors is simple — the ability to create the best products. "The market is crowded but still full of potential. Success is a sure thing so long as our products beat the others." said Eric Yuan, CEO of Zoom.

Eight years after founding Zoom, Eric Yuan ringed the Nasdaq opening bell on April 18, 2019. On that very day, its share price rocketed by 72% and market value surged to USD 16 billion. The reason Wall Street has been so optimistic about Zoom is closely related to its outstanding financial performance. Compared with videoconferencing giants that have

[3]All are video conferencing and instant messaging service companies.

suffered huge losses, Zoom stands out in this industry as one of the rare companies to be profitable. According to publicly available data, Zoom's revenue growth rate has consistently maintained a three-digit rate for seven fiscal years, from 2012 to 2019. As of 2020, Zoom had over 700,000 enterprise users. One third of the top 500 companies and 90% of the top 200 universities in the US are Zoom's clients.

What's behind Zoom's success?

(1) *"User-driven" genes*: In Zoom's official blog, Eric Yuan wrote about Zoom's values and product concept: "From the very first day of founding Zoom, we have been concentrating on providing users with convenient cloud videoconferencing solutions. It works as a guideline for all our innovation, cooperation, and other strategies. What we have gone through, grown up, and the honors and recognition we have received from the videoconferencing industry are attributable to our clients who are satisfied with our products."

Therefore, Zoom's quick response to user feedback has been key to it dominating the industry. Most of the time, the product team convenes meetings to collect feedback, and CEO Eric Yuan is also often involved in these feedback meetings. Since the time the product went online, he has logged into Zoom's official website nearly every day — he reviews users' comments and writes emails to every user who unsubscribed their service and asks them what they found to be unsatisfactory about Zoom's service. Based on user demand and feedback, the product team focuses on developing convenient and valuable video chat tools to solve any problem that their users face. With each iteration, new products continue to be based on user requirements. When Zoom found that individual users would like to convene large meetings, Zoom soon upgraded the 25-participant limit to up to 1,000; when enterprise users wanted to add social interaction, Zoom soon launched popular chat groups.

The principle of always putting users first enables Zoom to enjoy a high recommendation rate and user loyalty. In addition, with excellent technological support and the network effect generated by multi-people conferencing, Eric Yuan has led Zoom ahead of its peers. According to Sequoia Capital, an American venture capital firm, no enterprise prior to Zoom had possessed all the three advantages at the same time.

(2) *Building up the brand and reputation at high cost*: Zoom has always been dedicated to increasing brand exposure. "As a new service provider, we have to focus on those curious adventurers. It enables us to give full play to our biggest strength — user experience. If the early users like our product, they help us spread and promote the product." In 2016, Zoom signed a three-year deal with the Golden State Warriors (GSW), an American professional basketball team based in San Francisco, giving the team video conferencing technology to communicate with fans. In exchange, Zoom enjoyed substantial branding benefits via advertising in the arena (scoreboard, digital sign, etc.).

The combination of paid and free versions has also contributed a great deal in helping Zoom climb up the ladder to success. The free version generates traffic and reputation, while the paid versions generated revenue and profit. Zoom's video conferencing product is free for 40-minute-long meetings (studies found the ideal duration for a video conference is 45 minutes). But apparently, the 40-minute limit didn't stop people from giving it a shot. In fact, the free version has been widely accepted and favored by users.

"We wish users could give it a try. But the market is pretty crowded, so we can't say to them: 'Hey! You've got to try Zoom.' So, if we don't make a free version, they wouldn't even have a chance to try our product. The free version has done a really good job. It contains most of the features, and there is no limit for one-on-one meetings. That is why we have so many free users log in our website every day. If they like our product, they will soon subscribe and pay for the subscription." said Eric Yuan in an interview.

(3) *Scientific growth model and process*: The most frequently used or discussed traditional growth model is acquisition, activation, retention, revenue, and referral (AARRR). However, AARRR is in fact a linear funnel model — a process of quantitative one-time input–output ratio. Its edge lies in being quantitative, but the disadvantage is that it is difficult to view the growth process comprehensively and from a reuse perspective.

Zoom applies a "circle" growth strategy that highlights integrating resources and systemizing models. In many of the product integrations developed by Zoom, the key point is to place the retention triggers in the places or environments where users may need this product. Thus, the key to Zoom's development lies in environmental

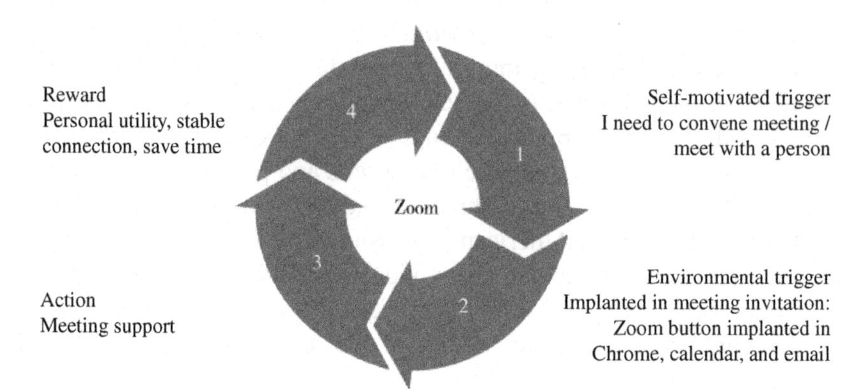

Fig. 3 Zoom's user habit circle.

Source: Qqchanpin (author: Shirley): Racking up over half of Baidu's market value in a month after going public; how did Zoom nail product growth? https://new.qq.com/omn/20190519/20190519A01M06.html?pgv_ref=aio2015&ptlan=2052.

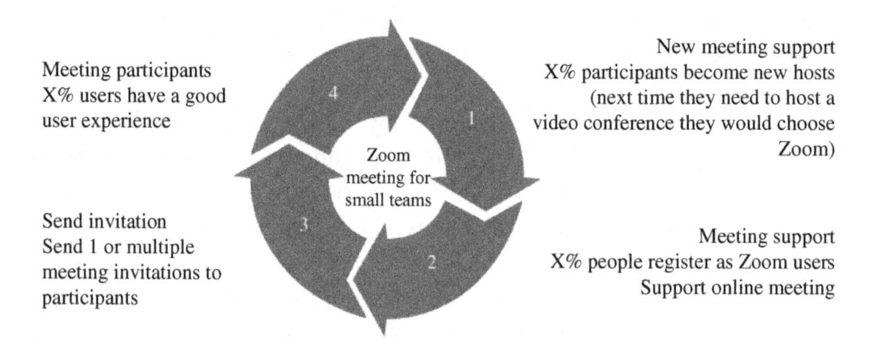

Fig. 4 Zoom's user spread circle.

Source: Qqchanpin (author: Shirley): Racking up over half of Baidu's market value in a month after going public; how does Zoom nail product growth? https://new.qq.com/omn/20190519/20190519A01M06.html?pgv_ref=aio2015&ptlan=2052.

factors. Demand for products like Zoom generally occur in the "upstream" — calendar, email, and chat applications. Moreover, Zoom cannot manipulate users' "meeting routine." So, to develop user habit, what Zoom needs to do is to place its product where users may need to use it and do it in a smooth and loss-free manner. Figure 3 shows the circle of forming user habits.

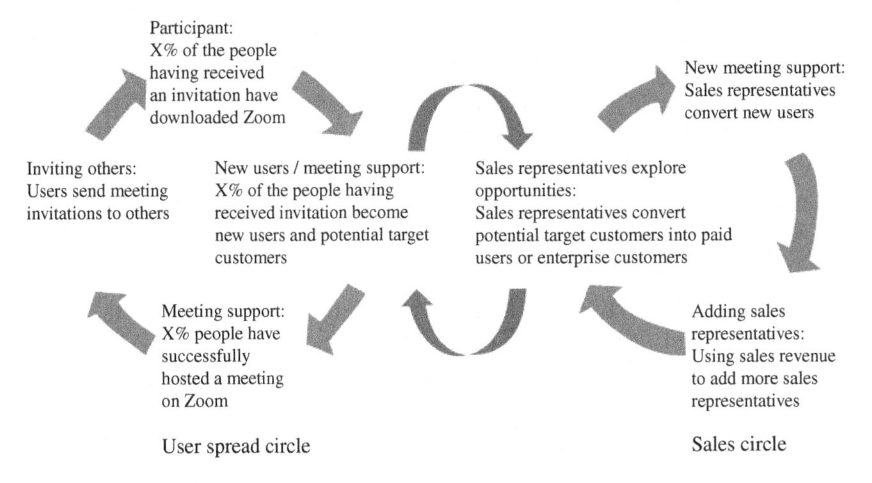

Fig. 5 Zoom's sales circle.

Source: Qqchanpin (author: Shirley): Racking up over half of Baidu's market value in a month after going public; how does Zoom nail product growth? https://new.qq.com/omn/20190519/20190519A01M06.html?pgv_ref=aio2015&ptlan=2052.

In Zoom's growth model, referrals work twice as effectively in user retention, as shown in Fig. 4.

As an enterprise product, the sales process is also relevant. Zoom has a large sales team as sales are a part of the circle towards developing a larger user base and final success, as shown in Fig. 5.

Zoom takes off again

In 2020, COVID-19 swept the entire globe — a nightmare that has adversely affected many companies and families. However, there are still some sectors and enterprises that have enjoyed excellent opportunities, such as mask-making enterprises, ventilator manufacturers, and video conferencing and teleconferencing solutions. Zoom is one of them.

Zoom is a typical provider of limitless supply products. Unlike vendors of limited supply products such as masks, Zoom can grow and branch out without any capacity constraint. Many people had to work from home due to the COVID-19 outbreak, and that was how many people encountered Zoom for the first time. After experiencing the ease of use, they recommended Zoom to their friends and colleagues.

During the outbreak, Zoom's DAU rocketed from 10 million in the end of 2019 to 200 million by the end of March 2020 and further to 300 million in April — a whopping 30 times more.

Among the new users, 190 million are free users. After the COVID-19 broke out, Zoom decided to provide free service to all newly registered Chinese users, and soon afterwards, it provided free service to educational and medical institutions across the US. In addition, Zoom canceled the 40 minutes limit, which was much appreciated in the education circle. Zoom also added social interaction features, which were particularly appreciated by the younger user group.

Although it is a videoconferencing app, Zoom soon became the top app on the App Store's free apps list, shocking everyone. Its market valuation bucked the trend of the declining industry. On April 28, 2020, Zoom reached a market valuation of USD 44 billion, nearly three times higher than the value on the day it went public.

Some may argue that it was luck that helped Zoom grab this great opportunity and grow its user base exponentially. It's true. But opportunity and luck work only for those who are well prepared. Zoom grabbed the opportunity and hasn't looked back since. This can be mostly attributed to its world-class products, excellent reputation, and smart marketing strategies. How many of Zoom's competitors saw their use base grow exponentially?

Chapter 6

Positive Feedback and Fission-Type Growth

Migration Cost and Lock-in Effect

The lock-in effect refers to a certain dependency on a product that users develop and at times unwillingness to use substitute products due to their habits and investment of time, money, and effort. The higher the migration cost, the stronger the lock-in effect. However, it is the opposite when the migration benefit is higher than the migration cost.

The core assets of traditional manufacturing enterprises are factories and equipment while those of limitless supply product vendors are technology, data, and customers. In this book, we have repeatedly highlighted the prime importance of users in the new economy: Limited supply economy is driven by production scale (capacity), while limitless supply economy is driven by demand scale (users). So, how to attract and retain users (reduce the churn rate)? In this chapter, we look at key effects influencing retention in the limitless supply economy, especially digital economy.

Let us first briefly introduce the lock-in effect. Here are some examples. We all have the feeling of inertia in our behavior, habits, and daily routines, and we need some time, someone, or something to give us a push to accept new things. Say a girl who was used to wearing flat-heeled shoes till she turned 20 would feel extremely uncomfortable if she had to wear 20-cm-high heels — she would not want to try wearing heels at all. So, without a strong motivation, she would not give up wearing flat-heeled shoes and turn to high heels. In the same way, iPhone users prefer a new iPhone with iOS rather than an Android smartphone produced by other brands. Lenovo users would also prefer another Lenovo laptop or desktop instead of Apple's Mac.

Users may take some time to learn and get familiar with products, especially complicated technology products. The time they have spent becomes their sunk cost. Switching to another product may need extra time and energy for them to learn and get familiar with the product. So, consumers don't easily give up the product they have been using to choose a substitute. For example, if you are accustomed to Stata[1] among all the software for statistics and data processing, you wouldn't spend time studying how to use Statistical Analysis System (SAS).

Purchasing devices and management software is also a huge cost for companies. If a company abandons all the original devices and switches to substitutes, the money spent on the old ones is sunk cost that cannot be recovered. For instance, if a company has spent a fortune installing enterprise resource planning (ERP) and office automation (OA) software, and if it now needs to switch to other systems or choose products and services from other providers, its previous efforts would have been in vain. So, companies, like customers, don't like to migrate products easily, unless there is a strong motivation.

In conclusion, lock-in effect refers to a certain dependency on a product that users develop and at times unwillingness to use substitute products without a strong motivation to do so due to their habits and investment of time, money, and effort.

Due to the lock-in effect, two identical or similar technology products may differ greatly in various aspects. The first one entered the market earlier and has accumulated a large user base and users become dependent on it. The second, however, is just a newcomer. Users who are quite familiar with the first product, would be unwilling to spend time learning and getting familiar with the second product. So, the second one may face the greatest threat — inability to obtain new users and thus fade away from the market. The early player has somehow "locked" other products of the same kind and developed the market based on this lock-in effect. This is also referred to as "path dependence."

---

[1] Stata, developed by StataCorp in the USA, is a world-renowned software package for data analysis, data management, and professional chart drawing.

W. Brian Arthur is a pioneering scholar who has studied path dependence in technological revolutions. According to Arthur, the adoption of innovative technologies is usually linked with increased returns. Thus, products that have been developed earlier can take the high ground and forge a virtuous circle that keeps building them up, thus defeating opponents. On the other hand, a better technology may enter the market late but get trapped in the dilemma of not having sufficient users or even get "locked" in a passive, vicious circle.

Lock-in effect further proves the importance of "taking the high ground" mentioned in the last chapter and provides companies a clue on how to retain users. However, lock-in effect may backfire or can be decoded, and its level may differ drastically for different products.

Decoding the lock-in effect lies on two key factors — migration cost and migration benefit. Migration cost deters customers from turning to other products or services and is the economic foundation of the lock-in effect. At the same time, migration income is the motivation. When the motivation is stronger than the resistance, the effect would be invalid.

Migration costs are divided into the following types:

(1) *Contract breaching cost*: In most cases, service contracts have a validity period. Terminating the contract before that date would result in losing the earnest money or a "breach of contract" claim. A common example is leasing a house. If you sign a three-year contract with your property owner and you suddenly want to cancel after only one year, you will be required to pay some compensation to the property owner. In other words, the tenants are locked-in by the contract.

(2) *Cost of device upgrade*: If you move to a new house, some of your old furniture may not be usable anymore, so you need to buy new ones to replace them.

(3) *Data transfer cost*: Transferring the contact list, messages, and other data from your old mobile phone to the new one takes time, which is a type of migration cost. If you want to register a new mobile number, you need to inform all your friends, colleagues, bank, etc., which is also a migration behavior.

(4) *Learning and training cost*: To understand the performance and usage of a new technology product, you need to spend some time going through the instructions, which involves learning and training cost. It is like spending time learning how to use home appliances and kitchenware that you just bought. It is just that when it comes to

technology products, software, or operating systems, this learning and training effort may cost more.

(5) *Vested interest loss*: Giving up old products and services leads to loss of vested interest. For example, if you use certain products for a long time, you can get loyal points to exchange for awards and prizes.
(6) *Psychological and invisible cost*: If you are accustomed to the community you live in and have made several friends, but you need to move to a new house far away, you would feel uncomfortable.
(7) *Migration income (cost)*: New products may have better features and quality, cheaper, and more convenient to use.

Lock-in effect provides a critical guarantee of customer stickiness (loyalty) and is of prime significance to internet or digital economy enterprises. Without it, all the fortune spent on attracting traffic and users may be in vain.

The strength of lock-in effect not only depends on the product's characteristics but can also be artificially generated. For instance, China Telecom used to lock old users by not allowing them to retain the number when they switched to other telecommunication service providers. Many old customers chose to remain as China Telecom users because they didn't want to deal with the inconvenience. E-commerce, banks, and airlines try to retain customers via customer loyalty programs, such as reward points. Airlines not only give customers "frequent flyer awards" but also provide high-end customers with gold or silver cards that include better services to lock them in.

Therefore, to decode the lock-in effect is extremely important for newcomers. Innovation, quality, performance, user friendliness, and price are all weapons that can be utilized to decode this effect, and innovation and product quality are the most significant weapons. If existing brands refuse to embrace new challenges and are unable to satisfy the diversified technology progress and user requirements, they can be brutally eliminated during each iteration. Motorola (MOTO) in the US and Nokia in Europe were once pioneers of the mobile phone industry, leading the whole sector from the 1990s to the beginning of the 21st century. In 2007, Apple released the first iPhone, leading to the popularity of touchscreen-based smartphones. Apple soon became the leader of the smartphone market, beating all the established mobile phone manufacturers. We also mentioned how Toutiao surpassed established web portals such as Sina and Sohu — Toutiao's magic weapon is technological innovation. From a dialectical point of view, Sina and Sohu withered as they failed to adapt to the trend of news and information push in the era of smart technology and mobile internet.

Network Effect in Smart and Digital Economy

In economics, network effect or network externality refers to a structure where a large user base leads to additional benefits for each user. In other words, it resembles the "Matthew effect" — the rich get richer and the poor get poorer. The competition in the market of internet-based industries is characterized by maxims such as "first-mover advantage" and "winner takes all."

The Network effect (Fig. 1) is a phenomenon whereby increased number of users or participants improve the value of goods or service. This effect was originally proposed by Theodore Vail for Bell Telephone, and was later popularized by Metcalf's Law stating that the value of network is proportional to the square of the number of the connected users.

Network effect was Systematically studied by the renowned Israeli economist, Oz Shy, in his 2001 book, *The Economics of Network Industries*. This theory explains how users of a certain product or

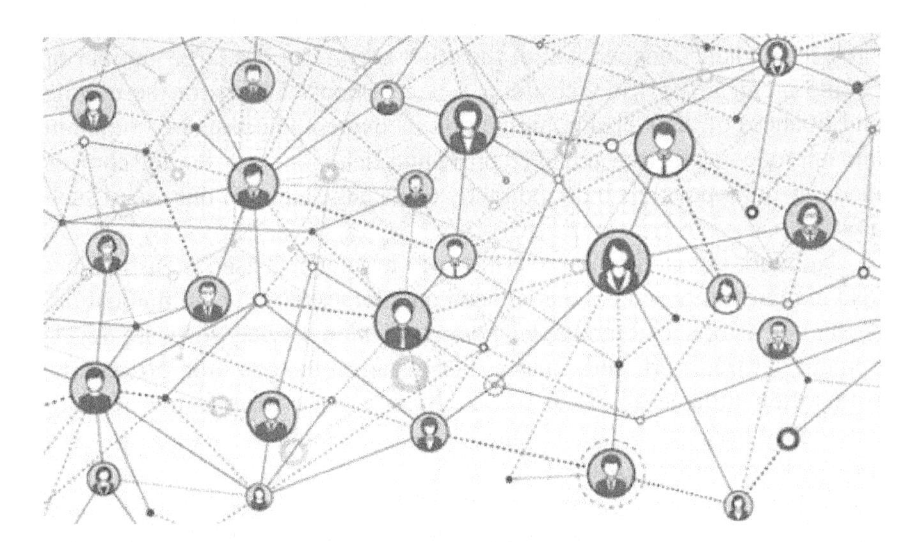

Fig. 1 Network effect.

Source: hulian.xiaob.org, taken from Baidu Image.

service remain interconnected in a network, and in doing so, the value of such a product or service is amplified directly by the number of people buying or utilizing it as well as by the compatible products introduced into the network. Simply put, the larger the user base, the more valuable the product, and inevitably the more beneficial it is to its users; that is, the bigger the network, the better the effect. In professional terms, the value of a certain product to a user is equal to the increasing function of the total user base of that product, which is also popularly known as network externality phenomenon in economics. For example, when people do not use telephones, purchasing one is deemed to be worthless; the more popular the telephones are, the more valuable owning a telephone would be.

In the real economic activity structure, multiple positives as well as negative network externalities are witnessed. If a scenic area becomes overcrowded and the tourists end up waiting in long exhausting lines for prolonged hours, people are able to neither enjoy the trip nor take photos. If a luxury product becomes excessively popular among the public, it leads to the depreciation in its value for conspicuous consumption.

There are two types of network effect: direct and indirect. Telephone users within a network are directly linked by the network effect, while the users of video hosting websites remain indirectly connected. In this manner, the activity of logging in and watching clips by a certain video website user remains independent of the other users. But if a large number of people prefer a specific website, it acts as a booster both for the morale and finances of the website, motivating its owners to constantly maintain and upgrade its services and keep providing richer content. So, the choices made by other people would indirectly elevate the value of our use of such a website.

Network effect is prominent not only in internet-based industries but also in many other sectors that depend on interaction and communication, such as news or social media, telecommunication service, software development, air transport, and finance. For instance, the common office software often utilized for text and chart processing also forms network externality because the final content produced using these diagrams and articles is not only to be used by the creator but can be shared with all. If you insist on using a proprietary software that no other software could decipher, then your work is deemed insignificant, and that is the reason why most people choose Microsoft's Word, Excel, and other universal word processing software.

Network effect is identical to the "Matthew effect" — the rich get richer and the poor get poorer. For internet-based industries, market competition is often illustrated by adages such as "first-mover advantage" and "winner takes all."

In August 2009, Sina Weibo, China's first microblogging platform was launched by Sina, a renowned internet company. After it was launched, Weibo swept the market with the explosive growth of its user base in no time. By the end of 2009, Weibo's active users had exceeded 5 million; by the end of August of the following year, the number of registered users had crossed 50 million. The instant success of Weibo encouraged many other internet giants back then to join the competition and create their own microblogging platforms. In April 2010, "Sohu Microblog" was officially launched as a public beta version. On May 1, 2010, "Tencent Weibo" was thrown open for users to register and invite friends. These products entered the market just a few months after Sina Weibo, but it was within these very months that Sina took the market by storm. Backed by strong lock-in and network effects, Sina Weibo took a huge lead in terms of influence, user base, revenue, and brand value. But of course, nothing is absolute. Tencent, learning from its previous failure, later invented WeChat, an innovative multi-purpose product for instant messaging, and grew by a huge margin over Sina in overall influence and user base.

Network effect is not just confined to the era of digital and smart economy but extends its amplified influence further as an inevitable trend in the new economy since the products, services, and users are interconnected. Further elucidating the same, individual products are linked with each other. Network effect demonstrates the demand-side economics of scale — the scale effect based on user base — an ideal foundation for developing limitless supply products in the era of new economy, since such products thrive with a larger user base and not by satisfying the diversified needs.

In fact, the strength of network effect is starkly reflected in the successes of Tencent and Microsoft. It is a widely held belief that they flourished due to technological progress. Undoubtedly, the operating system and office software, and social software and game development make an indispensable contribution to Microsoft and WeChat, respectively, but technology alone cannot fetch USD 1.2 trillion of market value to Microsoft and USD 460 billion to Tencent (as of the end of 2019). Microsoft and Tencent still have many counterparts whose R&D expenses do not even amount to about USD 10 billion. Hence, their success is largely derived from the network effect generated by a large user base as well as from the demand side economics of scale. By chance if one can even develop a social media application reasonably better than WeChat, it appears practically impossible to garner billions of users again.

The biggest value brought about by network effect is to strengthen the companies' ability of constantly drawing and maintaining users as well as their lock-in effect. Users are not only the core assets for vendors dealing with limitless supply products but are the very reason that unicorns are created. Industry giants seldom sustain by paying to acquire users for a long period of time because the cost is overwhelming. But for businesses thriving on network effect, it's quite the opposite — as the network keeps expanding, every participant is able to benefit from it, and the customer acquisition cost (CAC) either remains unaffected or even declines.

When Amazon was founded, it was neither favored by buyers nor by merchants; Amazon, back then, was nothing more than an online bookstore. But afterwards, it slowly progressed into a giant e-commerce platform, with annual sales volume of over USD 10 billion. Ever since, merchants all over the world have been jostling to partner with Amazon, and it costs them nothing.

Additionally, Amazon offers far more options and lower prices than Walmart, even with the home delivery service. Amazon's network effect offers solutions to effectively garner more users, boost profit rate, curtail CAC, and maximize the life time value (LTV) of a customer.

Today, a comprehensive review of the tycoons of new economy and their products, such as Microsoft's operating system and office software, Tencent's WeChat, Alibaba's Taobao, and ByteDance's Douyin, demonstrates that the network effect, direct or indirect, is highly instrumental for the new economy.

Products backed by a strong network effect also possess strong exclusivity, as incompatible products fail to connect with each other. For example, users of Sina Weibo and Tencent Weibo remain independent of each other and cannot directly interact. Hence, compatibility is the key to expand a network. It is the factor of compatibility that integrates the users of China Unicom and China Mobile and the users of mobile phones and landlines into a giant communication network via seamless connection.

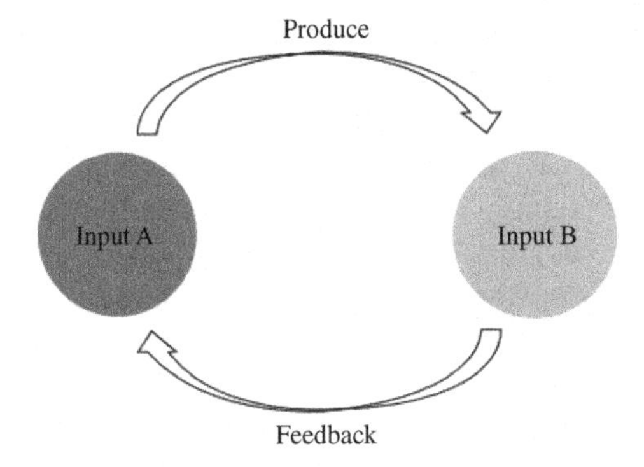

Fig. 2 Positive feedback diagram.

Positive Feedback and Fission-Type Growth

Another significant feature of digital economy, also known as internet economy, is the strong positive feedback effect — a substantial user base encourages businesses to upgrade their products and services every now and then, which in turn attracts more and more users. But only one or maybe a few winners can stand out in the fierce competition while jostling for market share with positive feedback effect. Positive feedback, therefore, essentially determines and drives the fission-type growth of companies.

Positive feedback signifies a structure where a systemic output affects the input — increased input results in increased output, which further triggers ever-expanding changes in the output. In simple terms, when A produces more B, B in turn produces more A, and vice versa. It is a ceaseless circle called positive feedback (Fig. 2). Positive feedback remains practically significant in nature, in human society, as well as in business circles.

Positive feedback effect and network effect share a lot of similarities; for this very reason, both are treated as special forms of the Matthew effect — "strong ones get stronger" and "winner takes all."

Digital or internet economy thrives on the strong positive feedback effect. But surviving fierce market competition is not everyone's forte and only a few survive it with positive feedback effect, as is most frequently seen in the internet economy. The bigger a network, the more valuable it is and thus is capable of garnering ever more users, service providers, and partners, thereby growing increasingly stronger.

In the online video hosting domain, platforms accommodate internet content providers (ICP) and the audience — also known as users. When the platform attracts many providers of video clips and other related content, it grows more popular, which in turn draws the attention of more and more users. Moreover, the more the number of users of a platform, the more valuable is the content of that platform, and consequently, more and more providers will be available to post and share other videos on the platform, thus forming a lucrative positive feedback system. Douyin, a video-sharing social media application founded by ByteDance, is a perfect example. Douyin, whose international version is known as TikTok, was officially released in September 2016. In 2019, it was rated as China's topmost film and television media brand in terms of brand value and soon became one of China's most popular short-video platforms with a huge international presence.

All e-commerce platforms specializing in B2C and C2C form another example. An e-commerce platform cannot develop without sellers and buyers. With more buyers, the business of merchants expands faster, which attracts even more merchants. Furthermore, with more merchants involved, goods tend to get more cost-effective and satisfactory in performance, which again results in more buyer interest. Alibaba's Taobao and Tmall rank as the biggest e-commerce platforms in China, and as a matter of fact, they are among the top ranking across the globe. They enjoy an unwavering presence globally due to their extremely large pool of worldwide buyers and merchants.

Positive feedback effect is also an evident part of technologies like software development. For instance, Microsoft's Windows OS tends to be the most frequently installed operating system on PCs. Whereas for mobile operating systems, Google's Android and Apple's iOS dominate the sector overall. They are, undeniably, top notch and reliable operating systems empowered by some of the most valuable brands but in no way can the imperative role played by a large user base be overlooked. A computer or a mobile phone isn't completely functional only with an operating system; it additionally requires a large number of supporting software or applications. A large user base of an operating system encourages more developers to create relevant applications. On witnessing an increase in the number of supporting software, more and more users prefer the corresponding operating system, thereby creating the positive feedback system.

For limitless supply products with zero marginal cost, the more the number of users, the more are the profits, and the products' vendor has increased capacity to invest funds in product R&D as well as to upgrade the product quality, which in turn attracts more users. Positive feedback effect is suitable for nearly all industries, especially those related to limitless supply products.

Furthermore, many such products function with a combination of lock-in effect, network effect, and positive feedback effect, making the market more prone to concentration and monopoly.

It appears noteworthy that positive effect, after all, is unable to equate to rapid and positive growth — it is a two-edged sword. It behaves like a magnifier that amplifies both advantages and disadvantages, while improving the winners' leading position and driving the others to fall behind the curve even more. In a nutshell, it makes the strong ones even stronger and the weak ones even weaker.

Since the 1980s, Microsoft has been a household name. Being a high-tech software corporation, it has managed to dominate the field of computer operating systems for decades now with its distinguishing features. On October 21, 2010, Microsoft officially released its mobile operating system, initially titled as Windows Phone 7.0. Afterwards, it was followed by a series of upgrades for the same. One of the most popular versions — which happens to be the last Windows upgrade version — was called Windows Phone 10. Mobile phone manufacturing giants, such as Nokia, Samsung, and Motorola, integrated Windows Phone into their respective products at one time.

Microsoft's expertise and strength in software development domain has always been unparalleled and it matched quite befittingly with Google and Apple back then both in terms of brand influence and overall strength. Then why did Microsoft suffer so terribly while competing against Google's Android and Apple's iOS? The answer lies in the parameters such as user base and positive feedback effect of the latter.

In comparison to the other two, Windows Phone was relatively a novice into the mobile phone market, owning a tiny market share at the beginning. Hence, with a marginal user base, Windows Phone failed to attract enough developers, mainly due to the absence of a proper app ecosystem and hardware manufacturing factories, thereby not proving a solid rival to the ecosystems possessed by Android or iOS.

Besides, Windows Phone lacked an all-inclusive ecosystem. Microsoft tried to encourage developers to join the Windows Phone ecosystem by funding them but to no avail. For that though, developers criticized Microsoft for modifying its mobile structure too often. Even from Windows Phone 8 to 8.1, major changes had been made to the system, depleting the developers' patience as well as confidence, which caused many of them to stop devoting their time for developing Microsoft's mobile applications and as a result made Windows Phone ever so weaker.

A small user base led to a flimsy ecosystem, which in turn, constricted the growth of the user base, creating a vicious circle for Windows Phone. In Q1 of 2017, a report from Internet Data Center (IDC) found that Windows Phone only accounted for 0.1% of the global market, but Android took up to 83.2% and iOS around 16.6%.

On December 10, 2019, Microsoft officially terminated its mobile operating system, stopped releasing new security upgrades, ceased the support for Windows Phone 10, and advised its users to switch to either iOS or Android mobile phones.

The so-called "nuclear fission" in physics is a typical example of positive feedback effect. It means an atom is bombarded by a neutron to produce a chain reaction, splitting a nucleus into several fragments, and then into several more, while releasing huge amounts of energy. This chain reaction, in marketing terms, is called a fission spread, a marketing technique quite common after Weibo and WeChat went public.

In the traditional economy, a person could only influence their friends and families. While in this age of social media, we can connect with anyone who may or may not share a similar hobby or interest with us to form a large social network. Compared to the information obtained from advertisements and other media adopted by business entities, people prefer to trust news that spreads within their immediate friend circle — a form of fission spread.

At present, majority of the successful marketing events and the exponential growth of user base for most of the companies has depended directly on user referral. Thus, enterprises need to give full play to market leverage to trigger the chain reactions that actuate the process of fission. Once a product gets forwarded by colleagues, friends, partner channels, or regular customers, the next level of promoters take over the baton and keep sharing and promoting it, where each user could bring in several new promoters, and this would lead to finally achieving the goal of elevating positive feedback effect to fission growth. However, if the sharing stops at a certain point, the chain is broken, leaving it incapable of triggering a fission and making the entire marketing event a festival for just a small group.

It is noteworthy that the lock-in effect, network effect, and positive feedback effect are all highly interconnected and interdependent. Lock-in effect retains users and enlarges the user base, followed by the generated network effect and positive feedback effect, which accelerate the growth of the user base to induce fission growth. Simultaneously, network effect causes the user growth to be a positive externality, which in turn intensifies the lock-in effect. In essence, positive feedback effect would stop functioning well without a strong lock-in effect paving the way. If enterprises fail to retain users, attraction methods, however excellent, would stop working after some time and would not trigger positive feedback from users.

Now, in Chapter 7, we look at how enterprises apply these marketing strategies to gain a competitive edge.

Chapter 7

From Product Competition to Ecosystem Strategy

Market Structure of Limitless Supply Products

The limitless supply product market does not form an ideally competitive market, hence it lacks large numbers of suppliers offering several homogeneous products. The natural evolution of such a market results in concentrated market power or a certain degree of monopoly or even oligopoly.

The two major differences between limitless supply and limited supply products determine the gap in the market structure as well as the market competition.

First, in the limited supply product market, each enterprise is constrained by capacity, hence they can only manufacture one product at a time, such as bread or beef, and to satisfy the huge demand, multiple companies are required to work at the same time. On the contrary, in the limitless supply product market, a single or a few enterprises can meet the market demand by introducing powerful and effective products like computer operating systems, search services like Baidu and Google, or social applications like WeChat. Therefore, it appears to be a complete waste of valuable time and resources if multiple enterprises compete by producing similar or identical products.

Second, for vendors of limited supply products, higher sales volume increases both the revenue and the cost, while for those of limitless supply products, higher sales volume can only bring higher revenue due to zero marginal cost. Without marginal cost and capacity constraints, a single company alone can satisfy the demand of all the users towards a certain product, and it becomes more encouraging and feasible to scale up or even monopolize.

In comparison, the desire for scale, market share, and even market monopoly of vendors of limitless supply products is much stronger and more realistic than vendors of limited supply products. Microsoft's operating system, Baidu and Google's search services, Facebook and Tencent's social network, and Alibaba's e-commerce service dominate the market in their respective segments.

According to microeconomics, there are four market structures — perfect competition, monopolistic competition, oligopoly, and monopoly — based on the number of enterprises, product differences, influence on prices, and entry barriers.

An ideal competitive market is a theoretical market structure where many enterprises produce a homogenous product, and each occupies a tiny market share. In the limitless supply world, such a market is neither possible nor necessary.

In a monopolistically competitive market, multiple merchants compete by producing diverse products. The competition seems fierce because a myriad of enterprises have easy access to the market, but the key that differentiates this market from the others is the way the enterprises gain monopoly status by offering distinctive products and services. To rephrase it, enterprises, if capable of producing distinctive products, can dominate the whole market competently. Therefore, in the case of a barrier-free market, market policies may inhibit the strength of individual enterprises. Online games, film and television, and music programs are all regarded as monopolistic competition markets, since each game or film can be treated as a limitless supply product. However, each game is specially designed and aimed at a certain group of targeted players; no single game can attract players from all genres.

An oligopoly market refers to a market where a few merchants acquire the majority of the market share. For example, China's e-commerce market is practically dominated by Alibaba, JD.com, Pinduoduo, and a few other internet giants; China's mobile payment market remains dominated by Tencent's WeChat Pay and Ant Financial Services Group's Alipay; and China's digital map service market is dominated by Baidu, Tencent, and Amap.

A monopolistic market is a market structure where only one company offers all the supplies. A monopolistic enterprise encounters a declining demand curve that the whole market suffers from. But at the same time, this monopoly not only controls the number of products the customers would have access to (even if the products can be replicated countless times) but also decides the price of these products. Microsoft has essentially monopolized the global market of computer operating systems and office software, while Baidu has monopolized the Chinese search service market (Qihoo 360, a Chinese internet security company, has a small share of the market as well).

Holistically, the limitless supply feature governs a higher market concentration, making the market prone to structures like monopoly or oligopoly. A single proficient enterprise can meet the supply demands of countless products, catering to the varied demands of all the users, and hence, emerging as the only winner. But in the limited supply market, winners lack a big appetite — capacity constraint. For example, even though Haidilao Hot Pot, a chain of hot pot restaurants, is highly popular, it is hardly able to monopolize the hot pot segment, let alone the whole catering industry.

In 2011, the "battle of the thousand group buying companies" or "the war of a thousand group coupons" took place.[1] Meituan, Nuomi (Baidu's group buying platform), and only a few other leading companies survived the battle. It is a typical case of how the limitless supply market has gradually transformed from complete competition to monopolistic competition.

In 2010, the Chinese online group buying market emerged. More and more entrepreneurs discovered easier access to the group buying market and believed they had a decent chance to succeed. They emulated a popular American startup called Groupon (founded in November 2008, specializing in online group buying). At its peak, China had about 5,000 companies, big or small, building group buying websites, among which Nuomi invested by Baidu, Meituan invested by Alibaba, and

---

[1] *Is Meituan Dianping's success temporary? Will Ele.me triumph Meituan?* Kuaibao, October 10, 2018, https://kuaibao.qq.com/s/20181010A12OXH00?refer=spider; *Review on "battle of the thousand group buying companies"; watch how Meituan's delivery service started*, Sohu, September 21, 2018, https://www.sohu.com/a/255235755_100141945; *Behind the success of Meituan is the failure of 1,000 similar enterprises*, Sohu, May 2, 2020, https://www.sohu.com/a/392570970_120419360.

Dazhong Dianping invested by Tencent were the top three enterprises. After the "battle," Meituan survived and turned to Tencent, and finally merged with Dazhong Dianping.

In 2011, the above-mentioned 5,000 websites initiated the infamous "battle of the thousand group buying companies," a rare event in China's internet history. During the battle, a boatload of websites left no stone unturned — raising funds from venture capital (VC) institutions, conducting an advertising blitzkrieg, and subsidizing the customers, so as to acquire maximum market share. At that time, they raised a total of RMB 7 billion. High-profile investors like lashou.com (a location-based, social commerce platform) and 24Quan (an e-commerce website focused on group buying) even provoked entrepreneurs with sayings like "march ahead as fast as you can; money is not a concern." In the end, they, of course, suffered a massive loss. Everyone was obsessed with spending money, resulting in a "prison dilemma" with no clear winner. After running out of all the funds, the majority of the group buying websites went broke and collapsed immediately in the face of fierce competition.

During 2010–2011, Meituan joined the battle, but several of its adopted strategies, which later proved to be correct and farsighted, facilitated its survival and prosperity.

(1) *Abandoning PC programs and turning to mobile internet*: In 2012, the majority of the players were striving to take over the PC market. Nevertheless, Meituan had the foresight to invest in food delivery — but as the economy developed, more and more people bought smartphones. So, Meituan gave up on the PC market and invested all his limited resources in developing mobile applications. They took a vital and resolute decision, as only two years later, in 2014, nearly 90% of the group buying orders were made through mobile phones.

(2) *Subsidizing premium merchants*: Several group buying companies and food-delivery platforms tried to attract users and increased cash flow with the launch of subsidy programs. Meituan, however, used these subsidies to take the higher ground of the supply domain, by partnering with premium merchants, and thus provided high-quality goods. Meituan managed to do more with less. For the PC market, subsidy seemed like an ineffective and hostile remedy, and the supply side was deemed as the fundamental solution. Meituan decided to subsidize premium merchants like Starbucks, Haagen-Dazs, and

Qing-Feng steamed buns restaurant and worked with them to draft and provide favorable promotions. Consequently, Meituan's market influence and customer satisfaction amplified, along with a certain rate of traffic conversion.

(3) *More targeted tracking data and information*: Meituan developed a specific tracker program. If a merchant received 1,000 orders per day, Meituan would check what the merchant did and how it did it. So, Meituan paid keen attention to where the money and the opportunities were.

(4) *Door-to-door selling*: Meituan hired numerous salespeople to visit each and every merchant, convincing them to join Meituan's ecosystem.

Finally, even without possessing advanced technologies but by simply applying entrepreneurial logic and effective competition strategies, Meituan evolved into a nearly monopolistic entity. In October 2015, Meituan controlled 50% of the food-delivery market and 80% of the group buying market. So, as an established monopolistic enterprise, Meituan raised merchant service fees from 2% all the way up to 12%. Evidently, Meituan's absolute monopolistic position in food delivery, alcohol, travel, and several other segments would by no means prove positive for merchants, delivery men, or consumers.

The "group buying battle" described above and the "trip battle" between emerging vehicle-hailing platforms like Didi and Kuaidi, reflect the brutal aspect of the limitless supply field and the digital economy. Without capacity constraints or even excessive suppliers, but with the phenomena like network effect and positive feedback effect, the market will eventually be taken over by a few leading enterprises, transforming it into a monopolistic market.

It is believed that the future of internet-based and digital-economy industries is a market structure called "721" — top 1 takes 70% market share. The next 2 take 20% while struggling to grow more, and the rest take 10% while facing critical struggles every day.

Diversification to Overtakes on the Corner

No vendor of limitless supply products with zero marginal cost can transcend the price competition by attaining an apparent cost (production) advantage. For the newcomers trying to decipher the first-mover advantage and lock-in effect to catch up with the market speed and even exceed it, the most powerful weapon remains the differentiation factor based on product innovation.

In the limited supply economy, any production decision or marketing strategy is primarily centered around one thing — cost or marginal cost. From automobile to clothing to catering, products at different levels, from different brands, and of diverse quality exist and flourish together. The reason is that the lower-level products come at a lower cost and are sold for a lower price; they take the market share they acquire through the price advantage generated by the cost advantage.

Nonetheless, no vendor of limitless supply products with zero marginal cost can stand out in price competition by gaining an apparent cost (production) advantage. WeChat, Baidu, and Toutiao all offer free services. Then how can newcomers beat them by the price factor? Will providing high subsidies help? Meanwhile, these leading enterprises are so well-established in the market that the others find it difficult to challenge both their capital pool and their overall strength. It is nearly impossible for any enterprise to use the low-price margin to snatch a share from Microsoft, although it charges hefty fees directly from users. Apart from user loyalty and trust, Microsoft also possesses the optional weapon of marking down its own products in the face of substantial threats.

In the previous chapter, we had discussed in detail about the lock-in effect and its significance in the limitless supply economy. If an enterprise desires to have a finger in the pie in the limitless supply market, it needs to decipher the lock-in effect of the leading enterprises. The key lies in increasing users' switching benefit over switching cost, by reducing prices and charges (or just subsidizing) or by increasing the utilization value of products.

Newcomers or small-sized enterprises find it extremely challenging to follow the operational steps of leading enterprises by manufacturing similar products and services, and then beat them via price competition or subsidies. Thus, their magical weapon seems to be product differentiation.

The lock-in effect is indeed a vital phenomenon, but not all products and services have a strong lock-in effect. For example, when most people received news and other information earlier, the source of the news, like Sina or Sohu, did not matter to them, and hence, both of them would have failed to enjoy a strong lock-in effect earlier with the PC programs. Thus, for limitless supply products without the presence of a strong lock-in effect, features like higher quality, stronger performance, etc., can enhance the competitiveness. Of course, the services being free (suppliers profit mainly from derivative yield) works extremely well. The perfect scenario would be a revolutionary innovation that amplifies the product performance and disrupts the existing industry. Now, to have a comprehensive sense of this, let's look at a few cases.

Case: How did Google surpass Microsoft?[2]

In 1998, the internet search engine giant "Google" was launched with an investment of around USD 100,000 by Sun Microsystems' co-founder Andy Bechtolsheim. But in the same year, Microsoft had already gained the status of a prevailing technological titan. The PC age could be primarily summarized with three words: Windows, Office, and PC, of which two of the parts were brought forth by Microsoft.

As the internet became popular and became part of people's daily lives, only two words caught the attention of Wall Street: content and service, due to which the startups like Google and Amazon were born. Google, small back then, did not appear as a direct rival to Microsoft and was not capable of threatening the latter's core interest, so it was not considered as a thorn on the side. Steve Ballmer, the CEO of Microsoft, once said that Microsoft's biggest mistake was relying on others' technology and failing to develop its own search engine. Thus, to create a new identity for Microsoft's search services, Live Search was officially replaced by Bing in May 2009. Bing had advanced to a huge extent, but was still unable to catch up with Google.

On August 19th, 2004, Google went public, raised around USD 1.7 billion, and was worth USD 27 billion in market value. After the Initial Public Offering (IPO), Google expanded its business beyond the search service and released new products like Google Docs and Google Maps, and started acquiring several startups. In 2005, Google bought a startup company called Android; in 2006, Google bought YouTube, then a novel video-sharing website, for around USD 1.65 billion in stock. A series of acquisitions and innovations expedited the Google rocket. At

[2]*Analysis: Battle between Microsoft and Google represents the battle of two ages*, Hangzhou.com.cn, September 8, 2005, https://it.hangzhou.com.cn/20050801/ca868733.htm; *Shaper of modern internet: a full review on the 20 years of development of Google*, https://www.cnbeta.com/articles/tech/765075.htm, and other public materials.

present, Google is a world-renowned technology giant on par with Microsoft, and in fact, much stronger than Microsoft in the fields of search engines, mobile operating systems (Android), and even the cutting-edge field of AI.

Case: How Toutiao overtook at the corner[3]

Toutiao's success is another case worthy of analysis and contemplation. Toutiao (literally "Headlines") or Jinri Toutiao (literally "Today's Headlines"), a Chinese news and information content platform, was founded by Zhang Yiming and a few others in 2012, several years post the launch of leading enterprises for information and news service, like Sina and Sohu. Based on his years of experience in the field of software development, entrepreneurship, as well as his unique judgment, Zhang Yiming chose a brand-new direction towards "content." Toutiao's team consists of 100 plus staff members — all of whom are mostly technicians, with no editors or news media specialists.

They focused on a single thing: aggregating valuable content from a large amount of news data via algorithm models to generate a tailored feed list of content for each user. Amidst the information outburst, the users were overloaded with a colossal amount of information. Toutiao stood out as a clear stream aiding people in focusing solely on the accurately tailored news.

The moment a piece of breaking news entered the market, Toutiao would manage to get a hold of it just seconds after and publish it immediately; faster than any other paper media and more precisely than any other news website for that matter.

This promptness and accuracy are the magical weapons that crowned Toutiao.

When it was officially launched in August 2014, Toutiao managed to accumulate over 10 million registered users within just 90 days. Before other competitors could react, Toutiao had already grown into a unicorn. In this manner, Toutiao pooled over 100 technicians and based on its unique algorithm and primitive AI technology, achieved something that essentially requires a team of thousands of professionals.

To tackle the problems of being a news aggregator, in 2013, Toutiao provided a self-publishing platform to media organizations. The platform

---

[3] *How did Toutiao take off? — Research on Zhang Yiming*, by Li Fang, Sohu, January 29, 2019, https://www.sohu.com/a/292112417_482521.

later evolved into Toutiaohao Account. Zhang Yiming invited more than 10,000 We-Media accounts to create content for Toutiaohao, leaving the trouble of infringement behind. Several months later, Toutiaohao had grown into one of the largest self-publishing platforms in China, second only to WeChat.

After 2016, content entrepreneurship and live streaming took off.

Since Tencent and Alibaba had their own ways, Zhang Yiming believed Toutiao must be able to pave its own way too. On one hand, Zhang Yiming invested in 30+ partners, including Tuchong.com (a leading Chinese photography community), Wallstreetcn.com (a financial news website and mobile application), Newrank.cn (a new platform for media service, social media evaluation, as well as advertising matching), Caixin Globus (a self-publishing media house focusing on international news), GeekPark (a Chinese community for innovators), Canyin Laoban Neican (insider reference for restaurant owners), 30sche.com (a news media website that provides automobile-related news), and even acquired Flipagram (an American short video company) and musical.ly (a music video company).

On the other hand, Zhang Yiming utilized RMB 1 billion to subsidize all the people creating content for Toutiaohao and launched two short video platforms — Huoshan (Hypstar) and Douyin (TikTok). Toutiao works as a news media platform, while Huoshan and Douyin serve as their social counterparts. By doing so, Toutiao progressed into a mammoth platform centered on internet content just within a few years.

Track-Seizing, Micro-Innovation, and Disruptive Innovation

Getting a hold of the market and constant innovation are the most common and effective strategies adopted by vendors of limitless supply products, to grow and compete. In terms of innovation, enterprises must consider product performance, and the compatibility of upgraded products, for self-disruption regardless of the possibility that the compatibility factor might not be beneficial for them.

For vendors of limitless supply products, once the products enter the market, the rarest resources are not supply factors like equipment and capacity, but are demand factors like users and market. Therefore, limitless supply product enterprises compete more fiercely to grab users and demand better than limited supply product enterprises.

(1) *Seizing the market and taking a stronghold*: A single limited supply enterprise, due to capacity constraints, can only meet a part of the market demand. Hence, this gives the newcomers a fair chance to develop, such as in the catering and clothing industry. The same is not true for the limitless supply market. Without capacity constraints, established enterprises can take over the whole market rapidly, meeting the diversified needs of the majority of the users. So, it becomes more challenging for newcomers to seize users from their predecessors. Given that, enterprises must be extremely sensitive to cutting-edge technologies and business models, dare to innovate, and seize the market to take the higher ground in the market competition. In the search engine segment, Google seized the market, and although Microsoft is a giant in the IT industry, it could not surpass Google in this segment.

(2) *Rapid expansion to seize the market*: Limitless supply enterprises usually grow faster than the limited supply ones — "fast fish eat slow fish" is a common trend in the new economy. If an enterprise is unable to capture the market quickly, it may be forced to face competition from the newcomers who rush in. Therefore, rapid expansion is a pivotal strategy for enterprises to explore new limitless supply markets, especially markets with a relatively low threshold to entry. Internet giants like Amazon publicly declared at the beginning of their rise that they were proud of burning money, were proud of not making profits, and aimed to capture the market share at all costs. In a *New York Times* article in 1997, Amazon announced: "We can profit. It may be the easiest thing in the world, and probably the dumbest. We are investing our potential profits in our future. No matter by which management level, it's the dumbest decision to let Amazon profit now." Many Chinese internet enterprises, such as Didi, Meituan, Mobike, Ofo, and Toutiao, adopted drastic strategies in their infancy to seize the users early and capture the market.

    Then again, burning money to implement such strategies may induce further risks or even cause massive disasters. Several internet enterprises, especially in the fields of O2O and sharing economy, crumbled due to the same. First, burning money on subsidy programs may trigger a financial crisis or a broken capital chain. Next, it may be exploited by deal hunters and every effort may be in vain. Lastly, users attracted by subsidy programs may not be loyal enough. Once the subsidy stops, they may probably turn to other products. In fact, risk prevention is not an overly complicated matter; it is fundamentally based on basic financial and business laws — balancing user value and Customer Acquisition Cost (CAC), and making efforts within your capability.

Prior to their merger, Didi and Kuaidi were trapped in a "prisoner's dilemma" triggered by such a strategy. In that battle of 2011, Tencent backed Didi while Alibaba backed Kuaidi. Tencent took the lead and funded RMB 200 million, trying to grab more market share at a lower cost. But on the very next day, Kuaidi worked with Alipay and released RMB 500 million as a subsidy — it applied the same strategy, only stronger. Ma Huateng (also known as Pony Ma, founder, Chairman, and CEO of Tencent) revealed in an internet meeting that Tencent invested a maximum of RMB 40 million in one day. But neither of them stopped, since everything would come to naught otherwise. It is said that to fight against Tencent and Didi's threat, Kuaidi and Alipay subsidized each driver and passenger RMB 10, endorsing the slogan "always one buck higher than the opponent." However, Tencent and Didi came up with a random red packet program that enclosed RMB 10–20. Several deal hunters located the loophole in that program and used computers, mobile phones, and other locating devices to repeatedly claim the red packets and profited a lot. After a year of ruthless competition, Didi and Kuaidi merged to optimize their profit together and obtain a win-win result. Didi spent RMB 1.4 billion and Kuaidi RMB 1 billion crushing down over 40 competitors. If it were not for their decision to merge, it is difficult to say when the competition would have ended.

(3) *Mergers & acquisitions (M&A)*: M&A is a key strategy for enterprises to form a league, to reduce competition, expand market share, consolidate the market position, and implement new technologies, products, and market segments. Didi and Kuaidi, as we introduced earlier, merged, and later Didi acquired Uber China. It was not very conducive to passengers, but by doing so, Didi managed to avoid fierce competition and consolidated its dominant position in the market. Many other industries have witnessed similar cases. For example, Meituan and Dazhong Dianping merged for the purpose of consolidating their market position. Google acquired Android to get their hands on cutting-edge technologies and products to further branch out to new and favorable market segments, which contributed immensely to Google's success.

(4) *Team-up (alliance)*: To function effectively, most limitless supply products need to be combined with supporting hardware and

software. For instance, video software needs to be installed on computers or mobile phones, along with corresponding operating systems. Facial recognition systems can only work when combined with lens and data processing chips. Manufacturers of limitless supply products, on being able to form an alliance with suppliers of complementary products and by implementing exclusive strategies against their opponents, are in a better position to consolidate their market position. Naturally, laws and regulations restricting unfair competition must be paid close attention to.

Since the 1980s, Microsoft and Intel have formed the Wintel alliance to facilitate the development of the PC industry. "Microsoft and Intel worked hand in hand to develop faster CPUs. Apple used to dominate the PC industry. But since IBM started using Intel's CPUs and Windows operating system in the 1980s, it replaced Apple and led the PC market. Microsoft and Intel also became major players of the industry," said Bill Gates, co-founder and CEO of Microsoft, as he described the friendship between the two enterprises.

From the 1980s to the 1990s, Wintel enjoyed its prime position. To work with Intel's CPUs with relatively large memory, Microsoft developed new Windows programs that utilized more memory, urging users to purchase PCs loaded with Intel's CPUs. Any other PC manufacturer, who previously chose only either of the Wintel members, in fact, chose to work with the whole alliance.

The nature of the Wintel alliance is not just reflected by its over 90% of the PC market share but also by how Intel's chips (hardware) perfectly integrated with Microsoft's Windows operating system and supporting programs (software) and were constantly upgraded together, eventually facilitating the entire PC industry.

Every time Microsoft releases an updated version of Windows, Intel upgrades its CPUs. Their cooperation gives a better user experience and an enhanced PC performance to customers of both brands.

The biggest achievement of the Wintel alliance till date was the battle against Power PC. In the early 1980s, Apple, IBM, and Motorola formed an alliance and jointly launched the Power PC microprocessor. The alliance was based on the approach that Apple would provide the operating system, and Motorola and IBM would work together on creating formidable Power PC chips, and the alliance would combine both software and hardware into final products for alliance members.

Wintel reacted fast. Intel released a game-changer — Pentium chips, and Microsoft released Windows 95. Both members of the Wintel alliance took separate actions to split up Power PC, but produced a collective effect which eventually caused the latter to crumble.

(5) *Micro-innovation or disruptive innovation*: In the era of a new economy where technologies, product quality, and features upgrade with each passing day, any enterprise that is complacent in innovating and keeping pace with the times is bound to lose its leading position. Innovation is an essential requirement that every business entity must face and study. Based on how much product characteristics and features get enhanced, innovation falls into two categories: micro-innovation or modified innovation, and disruptive or revolutionary innovation. Micro-innovation refers to upgrading iPhone 5 to iPhone X; revolutionary innovation suggests the innovations from LP records to audio cassettes and then to digital music. To make a decision on which innovation to embark on, enterprises must take factors like R&D input and technologies into consideration and pay close heed to how innovation influences its users. In other words, innovation appears contradictory to the very core of the lock-in effect and network externality.

While describing the lock-in effect in the last chapter, we had repeatedly highlighted the switching cost — the cost that users must bear when switching to other products. If the innovative products are highly compatible with old ones, the switching cost would be greatly minimized as poor compatibility leads to much higher switching costs. For example, it would be devastating if you cannot use your old programs, data, and documents in a new operating system. If a Word document that you wrote last year cannot be read by the latest version of Word, you will suffer a huge loss. If that happens, would you upgrade the software? Therefore, seeking revolutionary innovation without considering compatibility, can be too risky at times; and may not prove to be the best choice.

Poor compatibility also minimizes the network effect and its positive externality. Explaining further, if poor compatibility compels the users to willing switch to new products, it would not only hinder the promotion of new products but also segregate the users of old and new products into two distinctive groups or networks, cutting off their communication. Of course, every enterprise yearns to drastically innovate products to achieve higher performance as well as

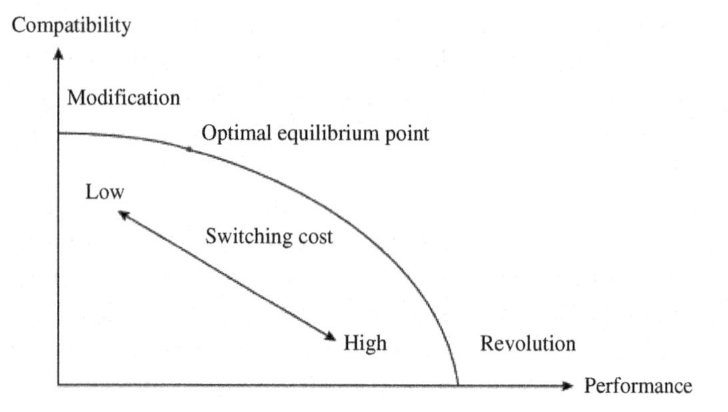

Fig. 1 Balance between performance and compatibility.

compatibility, but there are some technological limitations. Thus, enterprises need to strike a balance between compatibility and performance, maintain their leading role via technology, prevent the risk of disruption by external forces, aid in reducing users' switching cost, and avoid the lock-in effect from old products. As shown in Fig. 1, the optimal equilibrium point is jointly determined by factors like switching cost and internal and external technological environments. A stronger external disruptive force will only push the equilibrium point a little towards the side of performance improvement — tilting to the lower right along the curve. On the other hand, a higher switching cost means compatibility becomes more imperative, thus tilting the equilibrium point to the upper left of the curve.

Take Microsoft again for example. In 1995, Microsoft released the Windows 95 operating system — a revolutionary innovation of that time compared to its old Disk Operating System (DOS), but even so, Microsoft still considered compatibility. Afterward, Microsoft carried out modified innovations by upgrading Windows several times, from Windows 95 to Windows 98, to Windows 2000, and Windows XP — all highly compatible versions. Meanwhile, Tencent's innovation from QQ to WeChat was quite revolutionary. WeChat is not an upgraded version of QQ, but rather a brand-new social program. Old users can continue using QQ or choose to register a WeChat account while keeping their QQ account active.

(6) Driving out opponents and preventing their entry. To gain optimal profits, more market share, or even a monopolistic position, enterprises would like to drive out existing opponents and keep new ones out. Such

a strategy is usually applied by leading enterprises, and if this strategy works, it is even more significant for vendors of limitless supply products. The reason being that increased sales revenues can be entirely counted as profits. To achieve this, one can keep innovating and upgrading the products, to hold the higher ground in the market. Another tactic frequently mentioned in economic studies is applying an aggressive pricing strategy to scare newcomers away. The key to such an approach is sending out a strong signal to warn potential newcomers of your aggressive pricing. In addition, taking hold of the core stages of the supply chain and thereby dominating core assets of the entire industry also proves to be highly effective. For example, film and television companies can use exclusive contracts to keep (lock) A-list celebrities, and similarly, online education (paid knowledge) platforms can retain popular teachers — scaring away potential rivals or newcomers.

Case: Competition between Tencent and Toutiao[4]

In January 2019, WeChat enhanced the management of Toutiao-related products on its platform. To be more specific, WeChat stopped Toutiao's mini-program, blocked new Douyin users from registering with WeChat accounts, blocked the official website of ByteDance, and blocked the download URL of Duoshan (a video-based social messaging app). The battle lasted for over 8 months, and eventually Toutiao-related products became "big violators" on the WeChat platform.

In this battle, on one side, there was Tencent — one of the BAT (short for the three internet giants Baidu, Alibaba, and Tencent) and a king of social networking with 1 billion monthly active users, and on the other side was Toutiao — one of the fast-growing TMD (short for Toutiao, Meituan, and Didi). Why did they become deadly adversaries?

Eight-month-long battle that started from a short video

What lit the fuse to this "Tencent–Toutiao legal battle" was a short video

On May 8th, 2018, Zhang Yiming celebrated about Douyin becoming the world's most downloaded iPhone app in the first quarter of that year, by

[4] *When will the "Tencent–Toutiao legal battle" end?* By Yang Xuemei, Sina Technology, February 2, 2019, https://tech.sina.com.cn/i/2019-02-02/doc-ihqfskcp2522936.shtml.

sharing a video on his WeChat Moments, in which he further added that neither the move by WeChat to block nor to plagiarize Douyin, could stop the growth of Douyin. Ma Huateng replied to Zhang's WeChat Moment by posting a comment saying that "this can be considered as defamation, a lot of things need to be notarized."

Why did Zhang Yiming accuse WeChat of banning Toutiao products?

Prior to this, in March 2018, some WeChat users had found that they were unable to open the URLs of Douyin short videos shared by their friends in WeChat Moments. People assumed that "Tencent blocked Douyin." In fact, people could not open short videos of many short video platforms on WeChat Moments, including Douyin, Xigua, Kuaishou, and BoBoTV.

Toutiao characterized Tencent's action as an unfair trade practice — Tencent used the monopolistic position of WeChat to block Douyin and several other short video platforms, to develop its own short video platform — Weishi.

The "comment fight" in WeChat Moments kicked off the "Tencent–Toutiao legal battle"

In May 2018, WeChat released *WeChat External Links Content Management Specifications*, known as the strictest criteria restricting the spread of external links on WeChat. One of the terms was: external links must not distribute content containing audiovisual programs in any form without first obtaining the *License for Publication of Audio-Visual Programs through Information Network*.

As a result, at least 21 short video platforms (according to statistics), including Douyin, Douyin Huoshan version, Kuaishou, and even Tencent's own Weishi were affected.

The *License for Publication of Audio-Visual Programs* highlighted in the criteria is regulated and issued by the State Administration of Radio, Film and Television (SARFT). The license covers business categories of publication of self-produced programs, relaying programs, and provision of integrated operation service for programs. Institutions possessing the license are mostly central media, publishers, and local administrations of radio, film, and television. Not a lot of internet short video platforms possess this license.

Soon afterward, WeChat further updated the document, not strictly necessitating the license anymore, and announced that it will look deeper into the criteria with relevant program developers.

Users who wanted to share Douyin videos on WeChat had to download the video file to their mobile phone first and then upload it to WeChat. Kuaishou videos could be shared directly on WeChat, but only as URLs.

Besides the war of words, ByteDance and Tencent visited the court many times. On June 1st, 2018, Tencent announced that it had filed a lawsuit against Beijing ByteDance Technology Co., Ltd., the company that runs Toutiao and Douyin, and Beijing Microlive Vision Technology Co., Ltd. for unfair competition and serious impact on Tencent's reputation. In the meantime, Tencent also announced the suspension of cooperation with the above two companies.

On the same night, ByteDance replied: We have filed a suit against Tencent for unfair trade practices.

On June 5th, the Beijing Haidian District People's Court declared that Beijing ByteDance Technology had filed a lawsuit against Shenzhen Tencent Computer System Co. Ltd. for unfair trade practices and for blocking and banning users from visiting the Toutiao website via technological means, and asked the latter to discontinue its unfair trade practices at once, apologize, and compensate RMB 40 million for economic losses. On June 1st, the court accepted the case.

As competition intensifies, will Tencent completely block Toutiao-related products from WeChat's ecosystem?

The friction has been intensifying day by day, and ByteDance's products are gradually moving out of WeChat's ecosystem.

According to the notification, the Toutiao mini-program has been suspended due to its operation contents not complying with the selected category. No search result appears for the Toutiao mini-program on both iOS and Android versions of WeChat.

On January 23rd, 2019, new users of Douyin could not log in to the application using WeChat authorization.

Douyin assumed it was caused by glitches in the log-in service provided by WeChat. So, Douyin reminded users to bind their mobile phones to their accounts as quickly as possible, reporting that once WeChat bans login authorization, users may not be able to use cameras or other basic functions and may lose some already published videos, and also the DOU+ balance and other income.

Apart from that, WeChat also blocked the official website of ByteDance (https://bytedance.com); ByteDance claimed to be applying to Tencent for lifting the ban.

Later, on the night of January 26th, 2019, Tencent issued an announcement on the recent handling of induced violations and malicious confrontations. Multiple applications, including but not limited to Toutiao, Douyin Huoshan version, Xigua, and NetEase Cloud Music were penalized. While this was not specifically targeted at ByteDance, still many of ByteDance's applications were severely hit. As of February 1st, 2019, the official website of ByteDance remained banned on WeChat.

The battle between Tencent and Toutiao started in the circle of entertainment and news, but with the public launch of Duoshan, it expanded all the way to the social network, and in a much fiercer manner.

On January 15th, 2019, ByteDance launched its social networking application Duoshan. On the same day as the news conference, WeChat soon blocked the download URL of Duoshan. The same penalty was applied to another social networking application — MT. WeChat seemed to be extremely sensitive to any spread of new social networking applications in its own ecosystem.

"Don't take us as an opponent because we are working on different products. We only help customers connect with their closest people," said Chen Lin, CEO of Toutiao.

After the news conference, people assumed that these new social networking products were waging a war against WeChat. But Zhang Jun, director of public relations at Tencent, denounced them by saying "Randomly making something cannot challenge our supremacy at all. How can you call yourself a product if all you do is use red packets to attract users and trick them to download?"

Compared to Zhang Jun's blunt reply, Allen Zhang, the "Father of WeChat" had once said something about competitors in a WeChat open class, "We seldom think seriously about how to deal with competitors, because WeChat doesn't have any. We don't need to name a competitor for us. If we have a competitor, then it is ourselves, and whether our organizational ability can keep up with the changing times."

However, one undeniable fact remains that the social networking field has been silent and dormant for quite a long time. As time goes by, new products emerge, threatening the entire market structure. So, WeChat is naturally strengthening its defense.

Experts suggest network platforms are not regular subjects; they enjoy more and more public functions, and their increasing public functions, require them to shoulder responsibilities. Therefore, Tencent's blocking of other products appears as an unjust behavior, but probably for a righteous purpose.

Is the long-running bitter Tencent–Toutiao legal battle a battle for stock?

According to Quest Mobile (Beijing quest-mobile Info Tech Ltd.), short video and instant messaging are two market segments that contribute more than half of the overall increase in the use of mobile internet by users. Short videos, in particular, are a "black hole" that sucks up user time, having a 170% month-on-month growth in total use duration, surpassing online videos, and second only to instant messaging.

Tencent, however, was a newcomer to the short video segment.

In 2017, the first year of China's short video explosion, Douyin was among the pioneers. Weishi started chasing its predecessors in 2018 and tried to grab market share by sending red packets during Spring Festival, inviting celebrities, and by allocating generous subsidies to attract short video talents and multi-channel networks (MCN).

In the past year, Tencent launched 14 short video products, including Weishi, Shanka, QIM, DOV, MOKA, Mo Sheng, Tencent Cloud Short Video, Xiafan Video (video going with meals), Sukan Video (quick video), Shiguang (time) Short Video, yoo Video, Yintu, and Hapi. Apart from Weishi, yoo Video and Hapi, Tencent seemed to be putting an effort to branch out to the short video segment via various products.

Nonetheless, Toutiao's short video products maintained their stronghold so firmly that Weishi was unable to capture a significant market share in over a dozen months.

Quest Mobile's data suggests that Weishi ranked 6th in short video apps in December 2018, whereas three of the top 5 products are Toutiao's products.

Short video products are the base for young users. Insiders commented that "according to the user overlap ratio, the target customers of entertainment products are youngsters, and Tencent, one of the BATs, values young users very much." The short video had emerged as a major entertainment sector that sweeps young users' time. How could Tencent still remain calm?

ByteDance continued to try to enter the social networking field. If the battle had started with a short video, then the flame had spread to pan-entertainment distribution.

An industry insider said in an interview by Sina Technology, that users of smartphones are nearly saturated. The number of newly downloaded apps has increasingly been dropping. So, the next step for ByteDance is to take on the stock market to maintain its development. ByteDance has built firms with an ecosystem comprising of entertainment products. But such products die as fast as they arrive, leaving no room for consolidating a relationship chain. Hence, ByteDance needs to generate large numbers of new products.

Another interviewee, a post-millennial (generation Z) student, said that the youth watch short videos on QZone, and all the videos come from Weishi, and many others like to watch videos on Weibo. They feel it is unnecessary to download a Douyin or Weishi App. So, social networking and short video remain interdependent and intertwined.

Sina Technology found Douyin had been redirecting traffic for Duoshan by launching "Suipai (random filming)." A "random filming" video exists for 72 hours, can be commented on by private friends only, and then automatically disappears. Interestingly, it is quite identical to the "Shike video (moment video)" released in the latest version of WeChat.

Douyin "random filming"

Duoshan is building its own relationship chain via multiple resources and methods, and the key for Douyin and Duoshan to infiltrate WeChat is the latter's relationship chain — Contacts. If Duoshan successfully builds a relationship chain for ByteDance, it would be able to dig out more information about their users and users' close friends, and thereby create another WeChat — a short video version.

WeChat is nine years old now, so Duoshan still has a long way to go.

The Tencent-Toutiao legal battle seems to continue. According to Qian Hao, an internet analyst, as Tencent tightens control on access to WeChat platform, there could be more frictions like "Tencent-Toutiao battle." As for the user experience, Tencent's blocking tactic makes it harder for users to use other social networking apps, which could in a sense diminish their own user base. Nonetheless, banning behavior-inducing URLs actually facilitates the healthy development of WeChat's ecosystem.

However, a large amount of the population thinks WeChat would not completely "block" Toutiao's products. An article in *People's Daily* suggests that each internet giant desires to have a supreme market position, and retain a stronghold. There is nothing wrong with that. But the bottom line that they should not cross is abducting each other's users. Randomly blocking opponents would only trigger chaos across the market and eventually threaten the development of the entire internet industry.

Crossover and Ecosystem Competition

The multiple functions and attainable user (traffic) assets of limitless supply products make crossover operation a distinctive feature of the digital or internet economy. Competition among enterprises gradually transforms from individual enterprises fighting with each other by means of products into the contest of an ecosystem.

We had mentioned earlier in the characteristics of limitless supply products that such products can be used repeatedly without depreciation or loss, serve multiple functions, and bring handsome revenues for vendors. These features make crossover operation a favorable trend and an engine that boosts value creation for enterprises.

In fact, enterprises in the era of new economy do not focus only on specialization but also on crossover operation, for the following two reasons:

(1) Excellent vendors of limitless supply products do not suffer from capacity constraints that traditional industries like processing and manufacturing encounter. Thus, they grow rapidly and saturate their user base within a couple of years. At this point in time, a single product would not suffice to help the expansion of the enterprise. They ought to find new growth points to realize constant growth and fulfill the expectations of the investors.

(2) Crossover operation aids the enterprises to dig deeper into the user value. For all profit-making enterprises, users are always a critical part and the foundation for their survival and prosperity. However, as

we mentioned earlier, for vendors of limitless supply products or services, users are even more significant. For enterprises in the era of new economy, users not only buy their products or services but also "work" for them. For example, if you spend RMB 10 on bread, you contribute RMB 10 to sales, including RMB 1 to profit (if the production cost is RMB 9), then you have nothing else to do with the bread producer. But if you download and use WeChat, you become a user of Tencent who enjoys Tencent's products and services, but you are actually "working" for Tencent. This is because you are unknowingly helping Tencent earn its conversion fee, advertising fee, merchant promotion fee, interest on WeChat Balance, and service fee for withdrawal.

Since users are earning money for enterprises without being paid, the latter would wish to explore more channels to realize this revenue. Hence, if Tencent only focuses on social networking and game service, how can it generate enormous service and financial revenues? According to Tencent's 2019 annual financial report, it generated RMB 377.289 billion in full-year revenue, 21% year-over-year growth. Amongst all the income aspects, financial technology and enterprise service increased by 39%, the biggest yearly growth, to RMB 101.4 billion, nearly the same as the game revenue — RMB 114.7 billion.

It is crucial to highlight that crossover operation or diversified operation must be grounded in core competitive advantages of the enterprise, including technology, product, and user resource. Expansion, crossover operation, or diversified development not based on actual conditions and capabilities will lead to nowhere. Tencent and Alibaba branched out to the financial field successfully because they possess tremendously conducive internet technologies and products, and an enormous user base and user data — this is so valuable that the two companies together enjoy stronger and more unique competitive and innovation advantages than many other existing financial institutions.

In this era of new economy where everything is interconnected, it is nearly impossible for an individual enterprise to fight alone, to stand out and keep the higher ground. Enterprises must depend on many suppliers, service providers, logistics enterprises, partners, supporters, distributors, service objects, and user groups. They connect with these institutions, work together, and divide the labor; these institutions also connect with each other as a system with intertwined interests, which is better known as an ecosystem. To gain competitive advantages, enterprises must not only depend on their own products and technologies but also on the resources and strength of the ecosystem.

Wintel is an early example of an enterprise ecosystem. Netscape, a pioneer in the field of internet browsers was favored by Wall Street, but it failed miserably as it lacked a sound ecosystem. Netscape needed to function in Windows, while Microsoft was a tough competitor of Netscape.

In the last chapter, we introduced how Microsoft encountered its Waterloo in the mobile operating system segment. We believe this was because of the positive feedback effect. The reason positive feedback triggered a vicious circle is that Microsoft missed the chance of building a strong ecosystem for its mobile operating system.

"In the internet age, all enterprises need to build their ecosystems," suggested Zhang Ruimin in 2016, the Chairman of Haier Group (a Chinese multinational home appliances and consumer electronics company) and a "godfather" entrepreneur. In the future, every enterprise will transform from a closed environment into a node of the broad internet. Hence, they need to capitalize on the internet, take in and give full play to all sorts of resources, making the whole world their human resources and R&D department.

Jack Ma also announced quite early in Alibaba's development that Alibaba's mission is to make it easy to do business anywhere and everywhere. Alibaba's ecosystem is designed to make it convenient for SMEs to raise funds, conduct transactions and payments, and manage logistics. Alibaba can't help everyone on its own, so it built an ecosystem where each enterprise could locate its target users, enjoy logistics service, make fair transactions, and eventually flourish.

It is noteworthy that an ecosystem seems to be structured like grids, but at least so far, famous ecosystems have all been built around a core enterprise, aimed at satisfying the needs of the core enterprise in terms of competition and business expansion. This is the reason we often hear words like Alibaba-series, Tencent-series, Xiaomi-series, and Baidu-series. When SMEs join these ecosystems, they have access to necessary resources and assistance but can never position themselves as partners of the core enterprise. Centralization makes the ecosystem a closed structure, requiring all relevant players to take sides. Therefore, those who choose to follow Alibaba can hardly join and benefit from Tencent's ecosystem.

Case: Alibaba's ecosystem[5]

The ecosystem is a business competition circle, capable of expanding and intensifying, built via acquisition, teaming up and being open, and designed by an initiator to promote development, prevent competitors, and locate new profit points. As a top-level development model of the new economy, the battle of the ecosystem is like the Warring States period in the history of China. That is, traditional enterprises are destroyed and new giants fear to be replaced by newcomers. Thus, instead of newcomers grow wildly, the new giants recruit them into their ecosystem. As a result, the strong and big, swallow the weak and small, and the whole market is dominated by the "Seven Warring States."

Compared to traditional industries, internet industries have more useful light assets, less conversion cost, faster growth rate, more valuable

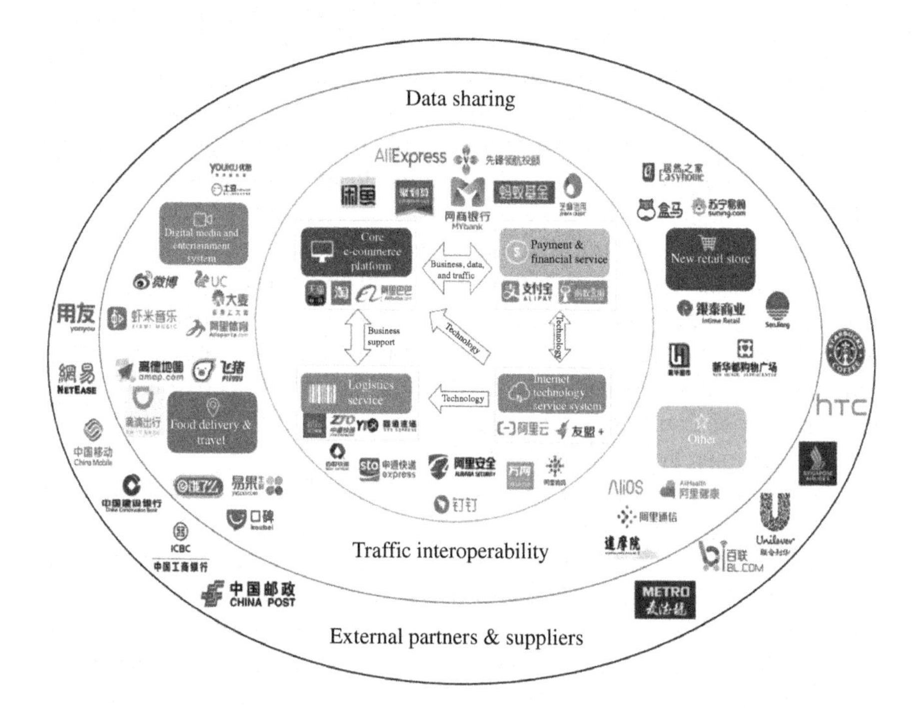

Fig. 2 Alibaba's ecosystem.

[5]Sorted by internet materials and public media reports.

users, and better cooperative effect among resources, technologies, and markets. This is the reason why in recent years internet giants have been carrying out diversified integration or cooperation methods, such as large-scale M&As and alliances.

Within an ecosystem, each enterprise holds a critical position. Instead of fighting for themselves, they depend on each other and strive for the same purpose, thus forming a closed circle — an imperative feature. This closed circle is like the Tai Chi Diagram that Jack Ma often refers to — harmony between Yin and Yang (positive and negative), virtuality and reality, black and white, demonstrating the essence of the art of business in integration and solidarity. Meanwhile, the fact that every enterprise holds its own position to battle against competitors, just like the troop formations to defend against enemies described in the ancient Art of War, vividly reflects the purpose of constructing an ecosystem.

Alibaba's ecosystem is based on its core e-commerce platforms like Taobao and Tmall. It keeps expanding and covers many new retail stores (Sanjiang Shopping Club, Intime Department Store, Suning.cn, etc.), food delivery, travel service (Ele.me, Didi, etc.), digital media and entertainment system (Youku, Tudou, Weibo, Alisports, etc.), internet technology service system (Alibaba Cloud, etc.), payment and financial service (Alipay, Ant Financial, etc.), logistics service, and numerous external partners, as shown in Fig. 2.

Chapter 8

Reflecting on New Policies in the Era of New Economy

From Rivalrous to Non-rivalrous

In the case of limitless supply products, there are no supply constraints; thus, there will be no scarcity of the product. As a result, such products fall under the category of non-rivalrous products. Whether non-rivalrous products are not restricted or restricted and charged depends on the business decision making and profit model arrangements of the enterprise.

Both consumption and business operation rely on resources and products. Different products and resources possess distinctive attributes as the product scarcity and sales or supply strategies of the suppliers may vary.

We hereby analyze the attributes of products (or resources) from the following two point of views:

(1) *Whether the consumption of a certain product is rivalrous*: The consumption of a certain resource or product is said to be rivalrous if once it has been consumed, then others cannot consume it, or if one consumes it more often, others can consume it less often. In short, a rivalrous product refers to a product for which more users lead to higher marginal costs, and the consumption of a certain number of products ensures others cannot consume the product at the same time. Examples of rivalrous products are gasoline, steel, cars, and PCs. Conversely, if a certain resource or product is non-rivalrous, no matter how much one exhausts it, others can still consume it as usual.

Examples of non-rivalrous products (items) include air and sunshine, Microsoft's office software, and Tencent's WeChat.

(2) *Whether the usage of a product is unrestricted and free, or restricted and chargeable*: If the consumption of products is unrestricted or is free of charge, they are unrestricted products; on the other hand, if the consumption of products is restricted (such as paid to use), they are restricted products. Bread and milk are restricted products, whereas urban roads are mostly unrestricted products. However, when it comes to software — Microsoft's operating systems are restricted products, whereas Tencent's WeChat is an unrestricted product.

Based on rivalry and restrictedness, products can be divided into four categories, as shown in Table 1.

Milk, bread, cars, and houses are private goods, whereas the VIP lounge of an airline is a shared good (club good). A free parking lot with limited stalls developed by the government for the convenience of people is a typical public resource, whereas TV programs of public TV stations and free applications (e.g., WeChat) are entirely public goods.

Normally, products developed by enterprises that have limited supply and are both rivalrous and restricted fall under the category of private goods. However, in case of limitless supply products, as they have zero marginal cost, they are non-rivalrous. Roughly speaking, most limited supply products are scarce due to capacity constraints and their consumption is also rivalrous; thus, they fall under the category of rivalrous products. Limitless supply products on the other hand do not have capacity constraints, they are not scarce, and are not rivalrous; thus, they are non-rivalrous products.

Whether non-rivalrous products are not restricted or restricted and charged depends on the business decision making and profit-model arrangements of the enterprise. Microsoft's operating systems and Tencent's WeChat are limitless supply products. However, the former is restricted and chargeable whereas the latter is unrestricted and free. As a

Table 1 Product attribute categories.

Attribute	Rivalrous	Non-rivalrous
Restricted	Private goods	Shared or club goods
Unrestricted	Public resources	(Pure) Public goods

result, Microsoft's operating systems fall under the category of club goods (after paying the software copyright fee, you become a member of the club and then you can access the product). On the other side, WeChat, developed by Tencent, a private enterprise, is categorized as a public good.

Tragedy and Comedy of the Commons

Due to their nature of being non-rivalrous, limitless supply products do not usually cause "tragedy of the commons." However, overcharging or excessive restrictedness would result in underuse, which in turn leads to the "tragedy of the anti-commons," whereas insufficient protection or inadequate restrictedness would result in insufficient production, which in turn leads to the tragedy of the quasi-commons.

The term "tragedy of the commons," or tragedy of public resources, was coined by Garrett Hardin in an article titled *The Tragedy of the Commons* published in Science in 1968.

Hardin made a practical example as follows:

A group of herders share a common parcel of land. Each herder wants to breed one more cow, as the benefit surpasses the cost, making it a good deal. But the average amount of grass grazed by each cow declines, which may decrease the unit revenue from cows in the entire pasture area. To sum up, every time a herder breeds one more cow, the grassland may be overgrazed and unable to feed all the cows, eventually causing all the cows to starve to death, which is called the "tragedy of the commons."

There are two ways to prevent it. First, systematic remedy — setting up a centralized authority, be it public or private (rendering the right of dealing with public resources to a private authority). Second, moral restraint, which is linked with decentralized rewards and punishment.

In practice, before it occurs, we can set up a set of values or a centralized authority which controls the number of cows by adjusting the cost or via other methods.

However, the "tragedy of the commons" is just a small part of the multiple and complicated economic problems in real life. For non-rivalrous products like limitless supply ones, there is no such thing as being protected from over-consumption — from the perspective of welfare economics, so long as users benefit from the product, it is a good thing. In other words, if a free and open grassland contains limitless grass resources (based on slightly modifying Hardin's hypothesis), then breeding more cows will not have any negative influence, and there would be no need for any intervention by a centralized authority.

Again, for non-rivalrous products such as limitless supply ones, overpricing or excessive restriction would result in underuse, thus leading to loss of social welfare — which is referred to as the "tragedy of the anti-commons." In 1998, Professor Michael Heller in the US proposed the theoretical model of "the tragedy of the anti-commons," in an article. According to Heller, Hardin's "tragedy of the commons" illustrates the consequences of over-consumption of public resources but neglects the possibility of underutilization of resources. On a common land, there may be too many right holders, and each of them has the right to set up barriers to block others from using a certain resource; as a consequence, when no one has the valid right to use, the resources are left idle or are underutilized, which results in in the waste of resources. Of course, even if there is one mighty player who has the right to set up extremely high barriers to block others from accessing the resources, it would still lead to the tragedy of underutilization of resources.

Although the marginal cost is nearly zero for limitless supply products, the early R&D and subsequent upgrade cost is comparatively high. So, for such products (club items), inadequate protection (e.g., rampant piracy) and restrictions would demotivate the enterprises' passion for innovation, thereby drastically reducing the number of club goods in the market. Such a situation is called the "tragedy of the quasi-commons."

As for those products that facilitate our work and life, such as Baidu's search engine, Tencent's WeChat, 360 Safeguard (an anti-virus program developed by Qihoo 360), and Youdao dictionary (a dictionary program developed by NetEase), which are non-rivalrous and there are no barriers on usage that have been pre-set by the developers excluding restrictions on violations or illegal behavior), then users of such products have unlimited access to these products. This is called the "comedy of the commons."

Policy Analysis in the New Economy Era

The concentration of industrial and market power in the field of limitless supply is normal in the new economy era. The formulation of laws, regulations, and economic policies needs to be able to balance the benefits of scale while preventing monopolistic power from becoming an obstacle to social innovation and the development of SMEs.

In the previous chapters, we concluded that the era of new economy will witness a huge surge in limitless supply products. The market for limitless supply of products presents several new features that are not available or are highly uncommon in the traditional product market from many aspects, such as the business operation methodology, revenue and cost composition, product pricing, market structure, and competition.

For instance, from the perspective of macro resource allocation and economic efficiency, it is undoubtedly an extreme waste of resources if many enterprises produce similar or identical limitless supply products. Therefore, it is reasonable and necessary to pursue economies of scale and moderate industrial concentration. However, excessive concentration will lead to the emergence of a "winners take all" phenomenon — common in the digital economy field. What is noteworthy is that the monopolistic position of leading companies in the new economy, especially the internet and big data industries, may no longer be limited to a market segment, as it becomes easier to conduct crossover operation and to branch out to other segments.

In the limitless supply market, capacity is no longer a constraint, innovation ability is pivotal, and user base is a core resource. Someone once said that for internet enterprises, "those who win the traffic win the market," which fully shows the significance of users. For enterprises in the new economy, users are no longer just the demand side of their products and services but are also their production resources. Leading enterprises can monopolize not only the supply of products but also users.

Frankly, concentration or even monopoly in the limitless supply market is, in a sense, necessary for enterprises to give full play to the scale and scope effects. The emergence of several leading large-scale internationally competitive enterprises in the field of new economy is also of positive significance for the development of a country's economy. However, the excessive concentration of market power would hinder fair competition, curb the innovation and development of SMEs, and have a negative impact on new entrepreneurs.

Therefore, the key issues countries in the era of new economy need to tackle are how to create a robust policy-making and law-enforcement environment and maintain a balance between the various pros and cons to help excellent enterprises branch out, enable SMEs to develop healthily, and encourage the younger generation to pursue entrepreneurship and innovation. The following are some preliminary thoughts on these issues and policy suggestions:

(1) In the era of new economy, technology and innovation are vital for economic development. The initial R&D cost of new technologies and products involve huge costs and risks; therefore, R&D personnel need to be motivated through sufficient compensation. That is why in the era of new economy and the internet, it is imperative to protect intellectual property rights to prevent the "tragedy of the quasi-commons."

(2) Enforcement of the *Anti-Monopoly Law of the People's Republic of China*, *Anti-Unfair Competition Law of the People's Republic of China*, and other laws and regulations related to economy needs to be enhanced to be in line with the features of the new economy, national economic growth, and to ensure public benefit in a bid to avoid the "tragedy of the commons" and to prevent abuse of market dominance and damage to the interests of users. Therefore, China must create a robust legal environment that supports fair market competition and the healthy development of enterprises, innovation, and entrepreneurship.

    The fact is that China is still lagging in legislation and law enforcement in the face of several unexpected issues brought about by the new economy. For example, Term 2 of Article 17 of the *Anti-Monopoly Law of the People's Republic of China* clearly prohibits business entities with a dominant position from "selling products at prices below cost without any justifiable cause." Now, looking back at the Didi–Kuaidi battle in 2014, we can find that the two platforms invested huge funds to grab market share and develop their own payment systems, eventually leading to the closure of dozens of other car-rental enterprises. Did their subsidy programs violate the *Anti-Monopoly Law*?

(3) Allocation of licenses and permits needs to be appropriate. A license is not a product of an enterprise. In a sense, it should be a public resource that must serve the public. It is critical to figure out how to appropriately allocate licenses or permits for key industries that must be licensed. So, what kind of enterprises are qualified to be licensed? Are licenses, as resources (especially rare licenses), biased towards large corporations? Licensing departments must formulate rules to guarantee that licensed enterprises serve other enterprises and the public and prevent them from seeking monopoly and excessive profits. Thus, we recommend that the Chinese government learn from

other countries on how to handle natural monopolies as well as how to handle enterprises that have acquired a monopolistic position via licenses or permits.

(4) Data, traffic sharing, and transactions need to be standardized. In the era of new economy, traffic and data are the core resources for enterprise development. In the internet sector, users lead to traffic and traffic leads to revenue. Most data are generated based on user behavior. In other words, users provide data — the raw material, whereas enterprises process data.

Most data are owned or controlled by a small group of large enterprises, which may not be good for developing the economy, supporting SMEs, or encouraging entrepreneurship and innovation. Amid the rapid development of big data and internet, it is of course extremely important to safeguard personal information and data security. Against this backdrop, how to create a fair and equitable market, lower the acquisition (referral) cost, guarantee appropriate information sharing, and curb large enterprises' dominance of data and traffic is an arduous challenge for government agencies.

Bibliography

[1] Agrawal, Ajay, Gans, Joshua S., and Goldfarb, Avi. (2019). Exploring the Impact of Artificial Intelligence: Prediction versus Judgment, Information Economics and Policy. *Elsevier*, Vol. 47(C), pp. 1–6. Amsterdam, Netherlands.

[2] Armstrong, Mark. (2006). Recent Developments in the Economics of Price Discrimination. Book chapter in *Advances in Economics and Econometrics*. Cambridge: Cambridge University Press.

[3] Benzell, Seth G. and Brynjolfsson, Erik. (2019). Digital abundance and scarce genius: Implications for wages, interest rates, and growth. *NBER Working Papers* 25585, National Bureau of Economic Research, Inc.

[4] Berger, Jonah. (2015). *Contagious: Why Things Catch On*. New York: Simon & Schuster Press.

[5] Brynjolfsson, Erik, Rock, Daniel, and Syverson, Chad. (2018). Artificial intelligence and the modern productivity paradox: A clash of expectations and statistics. NBER Chapters, In: Ajay Agrawal, Joshua Gans & Avi Goldfarb (Eds.), *The Economics of Artificial Intelligence: An Agenda*. National Bureau of Economic Research, Inc., pp. 23–57. Cambridge: USA.

[6] Byrne, David M., John, G. Fernald, and Marshall B. Reinsdorf. (2016). Does the United States have a productivity slowdown or a measurement problem? *Brookings Papers on Economic Activity*. Spring, pp. 109–182.

[7] Feldstein, Martin. (2015). The U.S. underestimates growth. *Wall Street Journal*, May 18. Online Article, https://www2.nber.org/feldstein/wsj05182015.pdf.

[8] Gehrig, Thomas and Stenbacka, Rune. (2005). Price discrimination, competition and antitrust. www.researchgate.net.

[9] Hadin, G. (1968). The tragedy of the commons. *Science*, 162, 1243–1248.

[10] Heller, Michael A. (1998). The tragedy of the anticommons: Property in the transition from Marx to markets. *Harvard Law Review*, 111(3), 621–688.
[11] Heller, Michael A. (Eds.) (2010). *Commons and Anticommons, Economic Approaches to Law*. Vol. 1. Cheltenham: Edward Elgar Publishing.
[12] Lewis, W. A. (1954). Economic development with unlimited supplies of labor. *Manchester School*, 22, 139–191.
[13] Peitz, Martin and Waldfogel, Joel (Eds.) (2012). *The Oxford Handbook of the Digital Economy*. Oxford, UK: Oxford University Press.
[14] Oz ShyA (2001). *The Economics of Network Industries*. Cambridge, UK: Cambridge University Press.
[15] Xu, Ji and Tang, Qi (2019). A review of literature on digital economy and national economic accounting. *Economic Developments*, 10, 117–131.
[16] Ling, Wei (2020). Research on quality evaluation and promotion strategy of digital economy development. *Open Journal of Business and Management*, 8, 932–942.
[17] Rifkin, Jeremy. (2014). *The Zero Marginal Cost Society: The Internet of Things, the Collaborative Commons, and the Eclipse of Capitalism*. Peking, China: Palgrave Macmillan. (中文版《零边际成本社会》, 中信出版社, 2017).
[18] Shapiro, Carl and Varian, Hal R. (1998). *Information Rules: A Strategic Guide to the Network Economy*. Peking, China: Harvard Business Review Press. (中文版《信息规则:网络经济的策略指导》, 中国人民大学出版社, 2017).
[19] Varian, Hal R. (2014). *Intermediate Microeconomics: A Modern Approach*. 9th Ed. Shanghai, China: W. W. Norton & Company. (中文版《微观经济学:现代观点》, 格致出版社, 上海人民出版社, 2015).
[20] Woetzel, Jonathan *et al. The Rising China's Digital Economy*. Shanghai: Shanghai Jiaotong University Press.
[21] Li, Fang (2019). How does Toutiao grow up? — Study on Zhang Yiming [EB/OL]. Sohu.com. https://www.sohu.com/a/292112417_482521.
[22] Li, Yunlong and Wang, Qian (2019). *Growth Thinking*. Beijing: CITIC Publishing House.
[23] Penenberg, Adam. (2013). *Viral Loop*. Zhejiang: Zhejiang People's Publishing House.
[24] Shi, Xiang and Yang, Jiawei (2019). *Fission Growth*. Beijing: Tsinghua University Press.
[25] Sun, Shifang and Zhou, Chaonan (2019). *Report on Digital Economy Conference*. Beijing: The Economic Daily Press.
[26] Duo, Yang (2015). *Fission: Create a Miracle of Dissemination of Product, Idea and Behavior under the Internet Thinking*. Beijing: China Machine Press.

[27] Yang, Xuemei (2019 February 02). When does the Tencent-Toutiao legal battle end? [EB/OL]. *Tech.sina.com*. https://tech.sina.com.cn/i/2019-02-02/doc-ihqfskcp2522936.shtml.

[28] Cyberspace Administration of China. (2018). Digital China construction and development report [EB/OL]. *Digital China Summit*. http://www.szzg.gov.cn/2019/szzg/gzdt/201905/t20190508_4871748.htm.

[29] Zhou, Chunsheng (2013). *Financing, Merger, Acquisitions and Corporation Control*. 3rd Ed. Beijing: Peking University Press.

[30] Zhou, Chunsheng (2019). *New Rules of Limitless Supply in the New Economy*. Caijing Magazine, Beijing: SEEC Media Group Ltd.

[31] Coker, Brent. (2019). *Viral Marketing*. Beijing: China Renmin University Press.

Appendix: Theories and Simple Models of Limitless Supply Economics

How Limitless Supply Overturns the Scarcity Hypothesis and Market Clearing

The homo economicus or economic man hypothesis, scarcity (limited resource) hypothesis, and market clearing hypothesis are three pillars of traditional economics, and the supply–demand relationship is the fundamental relationship in economic studies.

Homo economicus refers to an ideal man who is self-interested and rational and seeks to maximize personal interest. This maximization of interest is seen as the basic motivation for individual behavior (including individuals and enterprises). When a person (enterprise) faces multiple different choices in an economic activity, the preferred choice is the one that maximizes the interests, i.e., making a rational judgment and choice.

The scarcity hypothesis is considered as the very foundation of economics and is defined as the study of resource allocation. According to the scarcity hypothesis, economic resources or products and services manufactured to satisfy people's needs are always insufficient compared with people's countless desires (demands). In short, due to limited resources, humans can never produce enough products to satisfy all needs. Of course, resource scarcity generally refers to relevant scarcity — scarce compared relative to people's existing or potential needs, which, consequently, requires economic activities to be aimed at maximizing economic effect with minimum resource consumption. In conclusion, resource scarcity and people's desire to maximize economic effect with minimum consumption are the reasons why economics has been developed as an independent science.

The scarcity hypothesis has two interpretations. First, in a market economy, the use of resources is both exclusive and rivalrous. That is, enterprises pay a price to get the resources they desire but do not usually share the resources with others. Second, production consumes resources, and capacity is determined by how many resources are invested.

In classic economics theories, economists abstract the production factors (core resources) used in the production process into capital (K) and labor (L) and use a certain form of production function $f(K, L)$, such as the famous Cobb–Douglas production function, to describe the relationship between resource input and output (supply). Moreover, traditional manufacturers cannot suddenly change the limited capital input in the short term, so the marginal cost keeps increasing, sloping the supply curve upwards.

When the supply quantity (production volume) equals demand quantity, the market reaches equilibrium — the so-called market clearing. Otherwise, the market is in either a state of surplus (supply > demand) or shortage (supply < demand). At this point, the product price will be adjusted by the market mechanism, triggering modifications in product demand and supply (production volume), until the market reaches equilibrium.

The supply–demand relationship in traditional economics is established via a series of theories and deductions based on the three hypotheses mentioned above. Normally, if the price is the vertical axis (y-axis) and quantity the abscissa (x-axis), the demand curve is sloped downwards while the supply curve is sloped upwards, as shown in Fig. A1. The point where the supply and demand curves intersect is where market reaches equilibrium or market clearing.

According to the scarcity hypothesis, production consumes limited resources; therefore, products are scarce due to limited production capacity. The scarcity of resources is the core factor that determines the price of resources and the prices of products produced by using these resources. Although from a macro perspective, there is still a scarcity of resources in the new economic field, but at the micro level, there have been fundamental changes, whether it is the scarcity of resources or the scarcity of products.

Traditionally, production capacity used to be determined by resource input. One more product produced means one more resources consumed. The production of limitless supply products, such as smart and digital

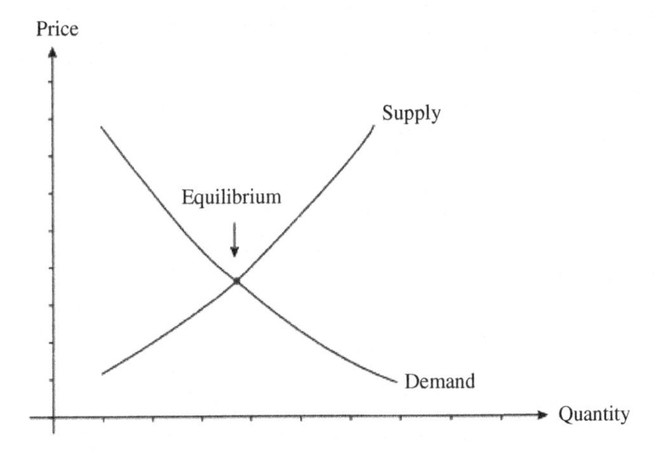

Fig. A1 Supply–demand curves in traditional economics.

products, e.g., software, consumes resources, e.g., labor force and energy, as well. However, once they are produced, they can be replicated at zero cost and sold to multiple users. So, such products can be supplied unlimitedly as needed till every demand is satisfied without additional capital or labor force (except for sales force, bandwidth, and marketing expense). The production functions derived from traditional economics to describe input–output relationship is valid in anticipating the production capacity of cars, food, and clothing but not meaningful at all in describing the number of copies of software, data, and audio and video products.

In terms of scarcity and rivalry, brand-new production factors, such as technology and data differ, fundamentally with traditional ones, such as land, capital, and labor force. The former are knowledge-based production factors that are always in short supply because at the macro level, the advancement of society leads to more innovative technologies and data, which in turn requires better technologies and data. However, at the micro level, any technology or data, once generated, will never be in short supply. Existing production factors can be used constantly without depreciation or used concurrently by multiple companies and individuals. Current technology or data, through which no matter how many products you produce, will never run out.

There is never a shortage of limitless supply products, there is no risk of inventory backlog, and there is no wastage due to surplus products as there is only one product — unless you cannot even sell a single product.

Therefore, the market clearing hypothesis in traditional economics is not applicable for limitless supply products of the new economy, or we can at least conclude that limitless supply products differ fundamentally from limited supply ones in market equilibrium.

Supply–Demand Analysis and Equilibrium Pricing of Limitless Supply Products

As shown in Fig. A1, the supply curve of traditional limited supply products is sloped upwards while that of limitless supply ones in the new economy is a horizontal line (as shown in Fig. A2). The demand curves are not as drastically different as supply curves (demand curves are sloped downwards in general), but they possess some new features. For instance, changes in market structure and competition pattern in turn affect the shape of the demand curve. Products and services, such as Mobike and Ofo's bicycle sharing, Mozilla's Firefox browser, Google's Chrome browser, Microsoft's IE browser, and Qihoo 360's 360 browser are highly interchangeable with one another, resulting in a fierce competition; hence, the demand curve is fairly smooth and the price elasticity is extremely high. At the same time, products and services, such as Microsoft's operating systems

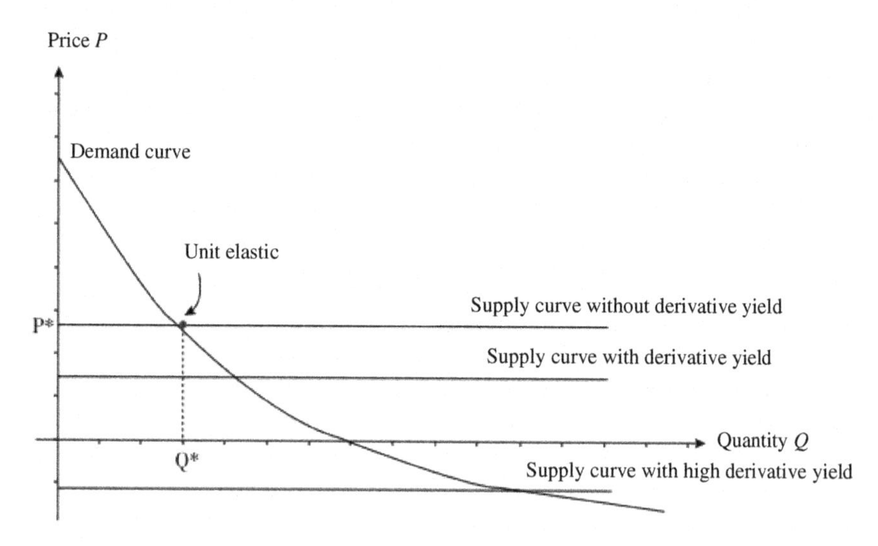

Fig. A2 Supply curve of limitless supply products in the new economy.

and Office software, nearly dominate the market; hence, the demand curve is extremely steep and the price elasticity drops sharply. Consequently, users are not that sensitive to the prices of Microsoft's products, but they are not completely insensitive. If Microsoft overprices its software and charges say several thousand dollars or even USD 10,000 per license, then a lot of people would not be able to afford a computer, thus lowering the sales volume of computers as well as operating systems and office software.

According to microeconomics, when marginal revenue (*MR*) equals marginal cost (*MC*), the profit is maximized. Therefore, when marginal revenue is at zero, the profit is at the maximum level. So, the question is when will an enterprise's marginal revenue be zero? Let's first clarify that zero marginal income (revenue) does not refer to either zero total sales revenue or zero average sales revenue; what it means is that the income obtained by adjusting the price to sell one more product is zero. The relationship between MR, price (*P*), and price elasticity of demand (*E*) as per microeconomics can be described as per the following equation:

$$MR = P\left(1 - \frac{1}{E}\right).$$

When demand elasticity equals one, i.e., unit elasticity at the demand curve, $MR = 0$, and the profit of limitless supply product vendors is maximum.

As shown in Fig. A2, the optimal price P^* of limitless supply products, i.e., the price that maximizes profit, corresponds to the point on the demand curve, where elasticity equals one. The corresponding demand quantity is the equilibrium quantity.

To make it easier to understand, let us assume that the demand function is linear:

$Q = a - bP$, where a and b are constants, Q is demand, and P represents price; then, the demand elasticity $E = \frac{bP}{a-bP}$. The optimal price or the equilibrium price is the price where $E = 1$. In numerical terms, $P^* = a/(2b)$, the equilibrium quantity (demand) is $Q^* = a/2$, and the corresponding (gross) profit equals $a^2/4b$.

It is worth mentioning that the two constants "*a*" and "*b*" are probably interdependent. Let us assume that a certain product can be sold in one area. When the product is sold for free, the number of users "*a*" is 10 million and "*b*" equals 10,000. So, every time the price increases by RMB 1, the number of users drops by 10,000 — 0.1% of the user base — when it is free. Now, if the product can be sold in two areas, the number of potential users, "*a*," increases to 20 million. So, it is obvious that every time the price goes up by RMB 1, the number of users drops by over 10,000. In other words, "*b*" would go up too. If there is no uncertainty about the demand in the two sales areas, then "*b*" will climb up to 20,000.

If we use "*c*" to present the represent the percentage of decrease in demand ("*a*" is the base number) every time the price increases by RMB 1, then $b = c \cdot a$. In this case, the linear demand function described earlier is as follows:

$$Q = a - bP = a(1 - c \cdot P).$$

So, equilibrium price $P^* = 1/(2c)$ and the maximum (gross) profit $= a/4c$.

In the above-mentioned linear demand function, we can interpret the constant "*a*" as the (potential) market scale of product, i.e., the exact demand when the product is sold for free. The constant "*c*" can be generally interpreted as the users' sensitivity (demand side) to price. Therefore, the price of limitless supply products is completely determined by parameter "*c*" on the demand side and has nothing to do with factors on the supply side. In addition, the profitability of enterprises is positively correlated with market scale (a) and negatively correlated with users' price sensitivity (c).

Influence of Derivative Yield on the Price of Limitless Supply Products

To analyze how derivative yield influences suppliers' sales and pricing strategies, let us first look at the linear model that was described in Chapter 5. Assuming that the demand curve is still linear, it can be expressed using the following equation:

$$Q = a - bP = a(1 - c \cdot P).$$

Let us assume that the derivative yield per unit user that the enterprise gains is d. From this, we can get the total revenue of the enterprise (*TR*, direct sales revenue plus total derivative yield) as follows:

$$TR = P \cdot Q + dQ = \left(\frac{a}{b} + d\right)Q - \frac{Q^2}{b}.$$

We can find the marginal revenue of products (*MR*, including derivative yield) using the following equation:

$$MR = \left(\frac{a}{b} + d\right) - \frac{2Q}{b} = \left(d - \frac{1}{c}\right) + 2P.$$

According to the marginal principle centered on profit maximization and assuming *MC* of limitless supply products equals zero, we find that when *MR* in the above equation equals zero, the corresponding price is the optimal price. In other words, the optimal price P^* of a product can be expressed as follows:

$$P^* = \frac{1}{2}\left(\frac{1}{c} - d\right).$$

Accordingly, the market equilibrium demand is

$$Q^* = \frac{a}{2}(1 + c \cdot d).$$

The above two formulas show that when the demand function is linear, enterprises spend half of their derivative yield for price subsidies, i.e., price reduction. Higher derivative yield leads to lower product price. When derivative yield from each user equals the reciprocal of the user's price sensitivity coefficient c, the product price is zero, i.e., it is provided for free. If derivative yield increases further, the price can be set as a negative number. In other words, to attract more users to earn higher derivative yield, enterprises can sell products for free and even issue extra subsidies to users.

As enterprises sometimes spend a part of the derivative yield on reducing the price, the sales (i.e., user base) will accordingly increase. Higher derivative yield leads to lower price and faster user growth. We can also conclude from the equation demand equilibrium that as consumers become more sensitive to prices (i.e., price sensitivity coefficient c increases), the price reduction strategy becomes more effective, leading to faster user growth.

Substituting the demand equilibrium and price equilibrium into the total revenue equation, we find that in the equilibrium state, the total realizable revenue (gross profit) of an enterprise is

$$TR^* = \frac{a}{4c} + \frac{ac \cdot d^2}{4} + \frac{a \cdot d}{2}.$$

The last two terms on the right of the equation are the increment in revenue (profit) generated by derivative yield. So, higher the derivative yield d from each user, higher the profit. However, we also find that as users' price sensitivity coefficient c increases, the driving force of price subsidy transformed from part of the derivative yield to stimulate demand, grows stronger. So, a higher price sensitivity coefficient c ensures the derivative yield has a stronger influence on increasing enterprise profit.

Economic Analysis of the Bundling of Limitless and Limited Supply Products

When complementary limited and limitless supply products are bundled, the limitless supply products can enhance the functionality and value of limited supply products. Hence, consumers are usually willing to pay higher prices for the final bundled product, i.e., the demand curve shifts to the right, according to economics theories.

For illustration purposes, we have used "*a*" as limited supply products, "*b*" as limitless supply products that are complementary to "*a*," and "*c*" as the final bundled "*a*" + "*b*" product. So, the demand curve of "*c*" — D_c, shifts to the right of the demand curve of "*a*" — D_a, as shown in Fig. A3.

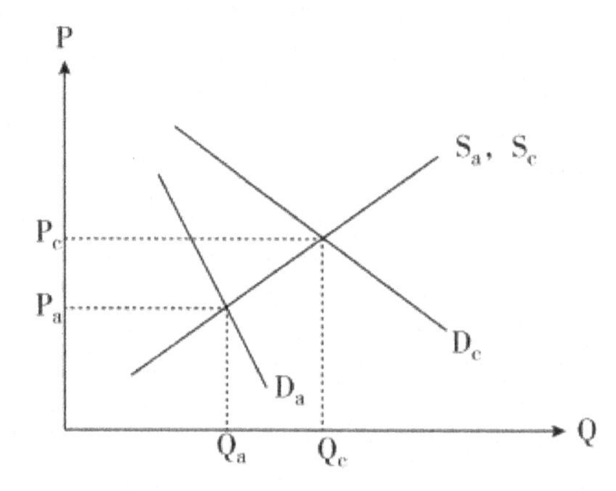

Fig. A3 Supply–demand relationship of bundled limitless and limited supply products.

If "*b*" has stronger functions, it becomes more important, and the demand curve shifts more drastically to the right, i.e., from D_a to D_c.

According to the basic principles of economics, if "*c*" is the superposition of "*a*" and "*b*," then the marginal cost of "*c*" — MC_c, should be equal to the sum of marginal cost of "*a*" — MC_a and marginal cost of "*b*" — MC_b. As the marginal cost of *b*, a limitless supply product is zero; hence,

$$MC_c = MC_a.$$

Again, as "*b*" has no capacity constraint, we can conclude that the supply curve of "*c*" — S_c and the supply curve of "*a*" — S_a overlap. Therefore, as shown in Fig. A3, thanks to "*b*," both the price and sales of "*c*" will be higher than those of "*a*" alone. This price difference reflects the added value of "*b*." Furthermore, after bundling with "*b*," "*a*" will be more attractive to users and enjoys increased sales.

Index

Printed in the United States
by Baker & Taylor Publisher Services